BAINES'S ACCOUNT OF THE WOOLLEN MANUFACTURE OF ENGLAND

With a new introduction by

K. G. PONTING

The text of Edward Baines's *Account of the Woollen Manufacture of England* is reprinted from Thomas Baines's *Yorkshire, Past and Present* (1875)

DAVID & CHARLES : NEWTON ABBOT

7153 4754 3

Set in 10-point Pilgrim on 12-point body
and printed in Great Britain
by W. J. Holman Limited Dawlish Devon
for David & Charles (Publishers) Limited
South Devon House Newton Abbot Devon

Contents

The text of Edward Baines's *Account of the Woollen Manufacture of England* has been reset but is exactly as the original except that on pages 77 and 79 the position of the tables has been slightly changed to fit the new page size

BAINES'S ACCOUNT OF THE WOOLLEN MANUFACTURE OF ENGLAND

Edward Baines (1800 - 1890)

Edward Baines, economist and journalist, was born at Leeds on 28 May 1800, being the second son of Edward Baines senior.

The elder Baines (1774-1848) had been a newspaper proprietor and part-time politician. He had bought *The Leeds Mercury* in 1801 and his work as editor played a leading part in the development of the provincial newspaper. Politically he was a strong Liberal, and it was in fact mainly due to him that Thomas Macaulay became MP for Leeds in 1832. Baines himself succeeded the great historian three years later. As a writer his *Lancashire* (recently reprinted) is important.

The son was educated at a private school in Leeds, then at the Protestant Dissenters Grammar School, Manchester, known sometimes as the New College; there John Dalton the eminent chemist was mathematics master. Baines early showed traits apparent in his later years by becoming a regular Sunday School teacher.

At fifteen he entered his father's newspaper as a reporter and was present at the Peterloo massacres; he became editor in 1818 and from that date wrote many of the leading articles. During these years he continued his self-education and became well informed on all political and social problems. In particular he visited a large number of cotton mills and lectured widely throughout the north. His first book was an account of the Lake District, but more important, he wrote the chapters on the Lancashire cotton trade for his father's volume and these were later enlarged to form his well-known work on that trade, still recognised as a standard authority.

He played a leading part in the formation of the Mechanics Institutes in the West Riding and this continued to be a major interest throughout his life. He presided at the Jubilee Meeting of the organisation in June 1887 three years before his death. Politically he was a very strong Liberal although not a member of the strict

Manchester school; he was returned as MP for Leeds in 1859 and made a number of speeches. He introduced Bills directed towards the reduction of the borough franchise and continued to represent Leeds until 1874 when he was defeated; he received a letter from Gladstone thanking him for the 'single minded devotion, courage of purpose, perfect integrity and ability 'with which he had discharged his duties. Baines then devoted himself to the public affairs of Yorkshire; he was knighted in 1880.

There is no biography of Baines but the *Dictionary of National Biography* has a very informative article. More recently W. H. Challoner in a bibliographical note to a new edition of Baines's *History of Cotton Manufacture in Great Britain* (Cass, 1968), draws attention to an unpublished thesis by J. R. Lowerson entitled 'The Political Career of Sir Edward Baines, 1800-1890', Leeds University, 1965.

INTRODUCTION

To understand Baines's account of the Yorkshire woollen and worsted trades in the nineteenth century, it is desirable to have an outline of the history of the industry up to that time.

THE MEDIEVAL PERIOD

The Cloth-Making Towns

During the Middle Ages the two chief cloth-making towns in Yorkshire were Beverley and York, although now there is little sign of cloth-making in either. Beverley was the more important, and almost certainly made better cloths. While the town's magnificent minster, the equal in beauty and size of all except the greatest English cathedrals, was being built, Beverley cloths ranked with those of Northampton and Stamford as the best made in England. All who attempt to trace the connection between the main centres of cloth-making in medieval times and the great churches then built will recognise the similarity between Beverley and Bristol, at that time the main centre of cloth-making in the West of England. Bristol's great days came later than those of Beverley, and the cloths made there were never so fine in quality as those from the northern centre, but the same connection can be seen between the cloth trade and church building. Thus Beverley Minster and St Mary Redcliffe, Bristol are outstanding memorials to the wealthy urban cloth-making industry, proving that the trade existed and prospered long before there was any question of foreign immigrants coming to either the West of England or to Yorkshire to teach it to the natives.

The other memorial to the cloth-making trade in Beverley is the so-called 'Law of the weavers and fullers of Beverley'. This document has been more fully discussed than any other medieval document relating to cloth-making in England, and it certainly stands in a class of its own. It dates from 1209 and is found with similar laws relating to the cloth trade in Winchester, Marlborough and Oxford. Writers have been considerably puzzled by these laws and as a result have differed in the way in which they have interpreted them. Most cloth was made for personal use, being spun and woven in villages throughout the land; it was only in cities such as Beverley, York, Northampton, Stamford, Winchester and Bristol where the trade was selling to a national or international market that the guild system established its full control with such laws.

In the villages and hamlets of the West Riding women continued to spin and men to weave, but we know little about these workers who, more than the urban proletariat of Beverley and York, were the ancestors of the future Yorkshire wool textile trade.

The 'Law of the weavers and fullers of Beverley' was short and can be quoted in full:[1]

> That they can dye no cloth nor go out of the town to do any trade; nor can any freeman be attainted by them, nor can they bear any witness; and if he wishes to forswear his craft he must do it to him who is called Mayor and the bailiffs of the town who will make him be received into the freedom of the town and turn the tools out of his house. And this law they have of the freedom of London as they say.

When one considers these regulations, it is important to distinguish between the guild merchant and the craft guild. The former came earlier and either were or became the city authorities. Leach, who edited the Beverley documents, stated 'The handicraft of which one hears earliest at Beverley was that of the weavers, which came about half a century or more after Archbishop Thurston gave his charter to the guild merchant'. The actual weavers' guild was first mentioned much later, in 1390, when it was named among the thirty-eight crafts who were to have a part in the play to be performed on Corpus Christi day. The complete working out of the connections between the guild merchant and craft guild is largely the work of continental scholars and was for many years somewhat ignored by most English writers. The fact that there was a merchant guild in Beverley suggests that this town closely followed the pattern of the great textile centres in the Low Countries, whose history Professor Pirenne has described.[2]

Professor Heaton interpreted the laws as enforcing an ostracism which could not be more complete.[3]

> Here evidently, a weaver was outside the pale of the burgess roll and merchant guild. So long as he remained a cloth-maker he had no caste in the town, he could not trade outside its walls, but must sell his pieces to the merchants who had probably made this rule for his imprisonment. The municipal courts of justice were closed to him and he could neither bring accusations nor bear witness against free citizens of the town.

This goes too far, and fails to distinguish between legal and industrial regulations. These laws were mainly concerned with the latter and did not carry the legal interpretations which Professor Heaton and other writers have given them.[4] Professor Carus-Wilson, the most distinguished historian to deal with them in detail, has stressed this industrial side.[5]

Earlier, some writers had suggested that the weavers and fullers had been foreigners, but there is no evidence for this, and the Yorkshire trade was founded on English labour and English skill. Writers wishing to find a basis for their view that the foreigners contributed anything can only point to a letter of 1336 where permission was granted to two weavers of Brabant to come to Beverley. The cloth trade, by that time, was at its peak and certainly the coming of two weavers could have had no effect.

The whole position is excellently explained by looking at the situation then applying to the Low Countries as described by Professor Pirenne. The merchant guild had originally come from that group of merchants who had first brought trade to the towns. Naturally they had to obtain protection from somebody, and the usual method was to obtain a charter from the king or a powerful nobleman, or alternatively, if the control of the particular area lay there, from the appropriate ecclesiastical body. Having obtained the charter to trade, they protected their rights. As trade increased so did the call for industrial workers and inevitably, some years after the formation of a powerful merchant guild, groups of craftsmen, following medieval traditions, began to form themselves into their own guilds. There was rivalry between the two, and the merchant guild, being the earlier, endeavoured to keep the newcomers subservient. This subservience, however, was far more industrial than legal; and this is the position that one sees behind the short but important laws of the weavers and fullers of Beverley.

There is nothing from York of equal value to that from Beverley, although reference to a weavers' guild comes earlier, having been granted by Henry II to the weavers of York at the same time as to those of London. The weavers' guild at York had a unique position amongst textile craft guilds in being founded by royal charter; the other guilds were based on municipal sanction, and were consequently more dependent than the weavers on the municipality, which one should really describe as the merchant guild, although in the case of York the legal formation of this body has been lost. Much has been made of this unusual status, but it is doubtful whether it ever amounted to very much or did any good to the weavers of York. The royal origin gave them—on paper—some control over weaving outside the city walls, but, as with so many other medieval grants, it is doubtful how far York was ever able to enforce it. Such control would never have been so complete as is sometimes stated to be the case; otherwise the great rural trade would not have developed. The weavers of York may have tried to make more of it than the actual documents ever implied, for the charter specifically excludes five Yorkshire towns and any other royal borough and, equally important, it covered only dyed or striped cloths.

The guild given by the king cost the weavers of York £10 a year, but they did not pay the sum regularly—whether because they found the advantages insufficient or whether because it was not collected regularly is not known. By 1224 the York weavers owed £180 and by 1236 this figure had risen to £210; in other words they were twenty-one years behind with the rent. In 1268 the sheriff of the county was told to go and distrain on the weavers for the whole debt.

The guild system dominated medieval industrial life, and in the cloth trade its control went far beyond the actual cloth-making; it extended to those who were ill, to burial of the dead, supporting religion and organising the celebrations on feast days. In addition —and there is little need to stress this aspect when writing about Yorkshire where the famous York plays are so well known—it did much to place English drama on the path that was to lead to the triumphs of Elizabethan times. As far as their supervision of cloth-working was concerned, the guilds attempted to ensure that the cloths were well made and produced by those who had been properly trained. There are no records from Yorkshire centres equal in interest to those from the West where at Bristol[6] one can trace in considerable detail the exact way in which this control was exercised, but there is little doubt that conditions were much the same in all cloth-making towns.

Yarn-making was relatively uncontrolled, but when it came to weaving, regulations stated that the looms must be in lower rooms so that anybody passing by could see that the work was done properly; it must not be carried on at night for the same reason. Even more careful regulations controlled fulling, and the fear beginning in medieval times that cloths would be imperfectly shrunk, consequently giving trouble later on, explains the emphasis on fulling in later centuries, when the state took over control of cloth-making. At Bristol the actual method of fulling was fixed, and here at least even moral questions were considered: no fuller was allowed to work in the pit with a woman unless she was his wife. Although later guild restrictions were to exert a harmful influence on the wool textile industry, there is little doubt that originally they did much to improve standards. The excellence of the cloths that came from Beverley and from the other urban centres depended upon this control, which was in fact a very real version of today's 'quality control'.

Cloth-Making Methods

It should be remembered that in medieval times, Yorkshire made only woollens. It was much later, in the eighteenth century (qv) that worsteds came to share and even dominate the scene. The detailed differences between woollen and worsted cloth are described on pages 37-42; for the present it is sufficient to note that worsteds are made from long combed wool, woollens from short carded wool. Both methods of preparing wool for spinning, ie carding and combing, go back to prehistory. For the moment, however, so far as Yorkshire is concerned, we need only consider carding.

Wool from the sheep's back contains various impurities and needs washing. The impurities divide into two groups: the natural wool fat contained in the fibre, which comes from the animal itself, and the dirt and vegetable impurities collected during growth. In practice both are removed but it is the second group that causes the trouble; if natural fat alone were present, it would not have to be removed before yarn manufacture.

In medieval times the washing or cleansing of the wool was done in any convenient stream, the normal practice doubtless being to place the wool in some type of container and lower it into the water, or to use the medieval equivalent of a bucket. Removal of the wool fat, itself a kind of soap, assists in the removal of the more difficult dirt, though the various vegetable impurities the sheep collects had to be picked out by hand.

After washing, wool becomes matted, and before spinning the individual fibres have to be disentangled and separated from one another—the carding process. The original hand cards were fitted with teasels; the carder held one in each hand and worked the wool between the two cards until all entanglements had been removed. At some time (the exact date has never been satisfactorily determined) the teasels were replaced by wires set in a leather foundation; these hand cards resembled those at present used in the industry for cleaning the modern carding sets. Carding and card-making were both well-known occupations in medieval times, and the word itself derives from the Latin name for teasel.

In the thirteenth century, at the time when the laws for Beverley were drawn up, all spinning would have been done with a distaff and spindle. Spinning wheels were unknown in England at the time, and comparatively rare before the end of the fourteenth century. Spinning consists of three distinct operations: drafting, twisting and winding-on. One of the differences between woollens and worsteds is that the former are spun with twist, the latter without —the twist being inserted later. But this particular difference was not completely defined until the changes in the spinning-wheel in the seventeenth and eighteenth centuries led to the full development of spinning with twist (see pages 38-9). Previously the hand spinners, using their fingers, could bring an almost infinite degree of variety to the process.

Taking a quantity of wool that the carder had prepared, the spinner put it on the distaff, from which it was gradually drawn by the fingers into a fine thread, any twist being inserted at the same

14

time—the shorter fibres obviously needed more twisting than the longer ones in order to avoid breakage. When she had made a certain amount of sliver in this way the spinner fixed its end to a notch at the top of the spindle. Then, when she had drawn out whatever length of yarn was most convenient, she revolved the spindle, thereby using it as a means of inserting whatever further twist she required. Finally she unhooked the yarn from the notch at the top of the spindle and wound it on to the spindle itself. The job was tedious but demanded considerable care if level yarn was to be produced. It is important to notice that the process was intermittent, even when long wools were being spun into worsted yarn; it was not until the development in the early sixteenth century of the so-called Saxony wheel with the Jurgen flyer fitted that yarn could be spun continuously. Anybody acquainted with the processes performed by the woollen mule in spinning today will recognise the similarity to the hand process.

Weaving was done on a hand loom basically similar to the one still used today. It had been developed over the centuries, and by the time of the great days of the urban cloth trade was a well-developed machine. During these years, in certain areas such as the West of England, the loom was considerably increased in size, becoming the so-called broadloom capable of weaving cloths 100 inches wide and needing two weavers. In Beverley, however, the cloths were narrow-width, needing only one weaver. He sat in front of his loom, threw the shuttle through the shed with one hand, and caught it with the other. There was no shuttle-picking mechanism in the modern sense; this only came with Kay's invention in the eighteenth century. The medieval loom consumed yarn much quicker than the hand spinners could produce it, and this shortage was a problem for the trade until the time of the Industrial Revolution.

Fulling was the most important finishing process. Most Yorkshire woollens were known as kerseys[7] and these had little other finishing; but it is unlikely that the better-quality cloths made in Beverley were similar to the kerseys, which towards the close of the Middle Ages were being made in other centres. We have no detailed knowledge of what Beverley cloths were like, but such evidence as exists suggests that they were expensive, and such cloths had usually undergone the important cloth-working processes of raising and shearing as well as fulling.

Fulling was usually done by placing the cloth in a pit and walking on it while in a wet state; the same result could be obtained by wringing it in the hands. Carding and spinning were women's work and were little regulated by guild restrictions. Weaving and fulling were done by men and were closely regulated; so too was combing and the combers' guilds were important in other areas.

The Rise of the Rural Industry

The rise of the rural West Riding woollen trade depended on the mechanisation of fulling and in this respect there were obvious and close similarities to the position in other cloth-making areas.[8] When dealing with the history of the woollen trade, fulling is a particularly interesting process as it was here that the earliest power-driven invention took place. During the Middle Ages the common method of obtaining power was the waterwheel; this invention was perhaps the most outstanding one made during the period usually known as the Dark Ages, lying between the fall of the Roman Empire and the rise of the New States in the West. By the tenth century the water-wheel was in common use for grinding corn, and there are many references to mills being used for this purpose in the Domesday Book.

It was a comparatively easy task to adapt such a waterwheel to give power for driving a fulling mill by attaching the wheel to a shaft which alternately raised and let fall a pair of heavy wooden hammers. The cloth was placed under these and thereby the action of human feet on the cloth was closely copied.

The development of the waterwheel for fulling had important effects on the location of the woollen trade. Previously woollen cloth had been manufactured in towns and had been closely regulated by guild restrictions, but the coming of this new type of fulling caused that trade to leave the old towns and go into any village situated on a stream that could provide the necessary water power. Regulations of the period are full of attempts made by the old cloth-making towns to prevent the adoption of the new method, whose advent has been described as an early industrial revolution.

During the years following the mechanisation of fulling, the tendency was to full cloths more and more, and in many areas heavily milled broadcloth became to an increasing extent the main production of the woollen trade. (In *Don Quixote* the noise of six huge fulling mills caused the hero great anxiety, but when Sancho Panza laughed the Don replied, 'It might happen as really it is that I had never seen a fulling mill before, though thou, like a base scoundrel as thou art, were born and brought up among such mean instruments of drudgery'.)

Among the earliest fulling mills in England was one in Yorkshire included in the survey of the Templars' land made in 1185. This was at Newsham, and incidentally lying outside the then-existing cloth-making area. The Templars were keen builders of fulling mills and had another at Barton near Temple Guiting in the Cotswolds. In Yorkshire there were early fulling mills at Almondbury, Alverthorpe, Bradford, Castleford, Kirkstall, Knaresborough, Leeds, Rothwell, Thorpe Arch and Wakefield. They were all the property of the lords of the manor, who found in this invention a welcome new source of income, so profitable that often when some measure of freedom was granted to tenants, the Lord of the Manor expressly reserved the right to maintain the fulling in his own hands. For instance, in the charter of 1228 granted by the Archbishop of York to Shireburn in Elmet, the burgesses in the borough of Shireburn 'were forbidden on pain of forfeiture to have an oven, pan or fulling stock'.[9] Those who made use of the Archbishop's dyepans might have in any week a cartload of dead wood at Shireburn. During the thirteenth century fulling mills spread rapidly through the valleys of the West Riding, and at Calverley, for example, there were at least five by 1257.

So the decline of the urban and the rise of the rural cloth trade began, aided and abetted by the love of restrictions now inherent in the guild system established in the towns. First of all came the financial burdens; the guild plays would have been worthy but expensive ventures. More important, the urban industry itself had become over-regulated. Authorities who attempt to control industry have always tended to overdo it; when they introduce a new, perhaps necessary regulation, they may forget to do away with what has become superfluous. Guild regulations meant that urban areas were unable to produce the cloths most wanted. Their decline

17

B

was hastened, too, by their unwillingness to introduce fulling mills; this stemmed from a variety of reasons, partly prejudice and partly the fact that satisfactory fulling mills needed the damming of rivers, which interfered with transport. The guilds continued on their downward track, halting at intervals to issue new ordinances which were as vigorous in language as they were ineffective in action.[10] When Leland came to Beverley he found 'that there had been good cloth-making there . . . it was now much decayed'.

The same course of events took place in York. A late document of 1561 stated:

> And the cause of the decay of the said weavers and looms for woollens within the said city as I do understand and learn is the lack of cloth-making in the said city as was in old time accustomed, which is now increased and used in the towns of Halifax, Leeds and Wakefield for that not only the commodity of the water mills is there nigh at hand but also the poor folk as spinners, carders and other necessary work-people for the said webbing may there besides their hand labour have rye, fire and other relief good cheap, which is in the city very dear and wanting.[11]

No one could have put the position more clearly.

The expansion of the rural trade in the West Riding of Yorkshire has been little described and the signs of it are now less apparent than, for example, in the West of England, where the industrial expansion of the early nineteenth century was not sufficient to cover up the physical signs of this early industrial revolution. Nevertheless, it was during these years that the West Riding woollen trade was founded in the area lying south and west of Leeds.

The aulnage accounts[12] give some indication of the new trade, but they can only be used to a limited extent for two reasons. First the accounts were usually inaccurate; aulnagers often inserted whatever figures they felt inclined to and consequently, even in the West of England where most cloths were subject to them, they can only be used with the greatest caution. The other reason is more peculiar to Yorkshire. By the famous statute of Edward III only cloths of above half a cloth of assize were subject to aulnage and as far as the West Riding clothiers made kerseys which were only equal to a quarter of a cloth they were not, at that time, chargeable. In 1393-4 a new law was passed declaring that any weaver might 'make and put to sale cloths as well as kerseys and others of such length and breadth as him shall please paying the subsidy, aulnage and other duties on every piece of cloth after the rate of the size of cloth mentioned in the statute of Edward III, that is in proportion to the size of the pieces'. This Act clearly made the smaller pieces liable to the subsidy, which on cloths of assize was 4d. The kersey was about equal to one-quarter of a standard cloth and therefore the levy on these shorter and narrower Yorkshire pieces was 1d; it remained at that figure as long as the aulnage system continued.[13]

Although it is impossible to use the aulnage accounts as a reliable guide to the West Riding trade they do indicate its growth and show that whatever the actual size of the industry, the West Riding was no longer economically isolated. For many years the district had been poor and outside the scope of the vision of the central authorities. Towards the end of the medieval period, however, this was changing, and Northern Dozens and Yorkshire Kerseys, better made than before owing to the increased fulling in the water-driven mills, were being bought by people throughout the country—by the monks of Durham and the choristers of Cambridge. Some were even beginning to go to Blackwell Hall *en route* for the markets of Europe. The valleys of the West Riding for the first time were playing their part in the economic and industrial life of the country.

It is still not always realised to what extent the West Riding had become one of the main cloth-making areas of England in the fifteenth century. Taking figures based upon years in the last decades of that century and reducing them to a twelve-month basis, Professor Heaton obtained the following figures:[14]

	No of cloths
Suffolk	5,188
Somerset	4,981
Yorkshire City and County (mostly from the West Riding)	4,972
Bristol and Gloucester	4,874
Wiltshire	4,310

THE TUDOR PERIOD

The growth of the Yorkshire woollen trade during the last decades of the Middle Ages meant that by the beginning of the Tudor dynasty it had become one of the three great cloth-making areas of the country. None of the cloths made there compared in fame and value with the Westcountry broadcloth, but taken as a whole the area's production probably compared in quantity, if not in quality, with that from the better known cloth-making centres of East Anglia.

It is sometimes stated that the reason for the inferiority of the Yorkshire cloths was the fact that the clothiers there were less successful or less highly skilled than those in the West—that in fact they used the same wool but could not turn it into as good a cloth. This is not true. The Yorkshire kerseys were made from local wool, coarse but hard-wearing. It made up excellently but admittedly lacked the finer qualities of the Westcountry broadcloth, which was manufactured from the best wools in the country, notably the famous 'Leominster Ore' from Herefordshire. In addition, the Westcountry clothiers devoted more time to the fulling and produced a heavier, more felted, fabric. Nevertheless, for the day-to-day wear of the average Englishman the Yorkshire kersey was probably as good as anything made at that time.

Throughout the cloth-making areas of England the Tudor period saw the final establishment of what has long been known as the 'domestic system', a term sometimes used so vaguely as to mean only the system under which industry operated between the decay of the guild and the coming of the factory. Even this definition is not quite satisfactory, for there were Tudor factories such as the famous one of Jack of Newbury, and that of William Stump of Malmesbury in Wiltshire; there had been something approaching the same thing in that of Hodgkin of Halifax. But generally these can be ignored and too much has been made of them because the factory system finally triumphed. The statute of 1555 has been described as the Anti-factory Act, but this overstates the case. The advantage of collecting workers together was that a certain amount of waste could be saved by better supervision and by preventing the petty thieving that must have been common under the domestic system. Nevertheless, the advantages were slight and when it was found that the Government, for a variety of reasons, was opposed to this development, clothiers in all areas dropped it without losing much.[15]

There have been many attempts to define the difference between the domestic system in the West of England and in Yorkshire—was it fundamental or merely a matter of degree? One might perhaps point out that difference of degree can become fundamental, as in the case of the super-market and the village store although they are both in the same business—retailing. Certainly the domestic system in the two areas showed fundamental differences, which accounted for much of the divergence in their future development.

In both areas the workers owned the machines on which they worked, but in Yorkshire, unlike in the West, they also owned the materials. Professor Heaton, in his well-known book on the Yorkshire trade, seems to underestimate the differences this involved when he writes:

> Thus the way in which the clothiers spent their time largely depended on the extent of their output, and the differences between the character of the Yorkshire and the West of England clothiers so frequently commented upon by economic historians was entirely due to the difference in degree of operation. . . .
> The report of the Parliamentary Committee of 1806 created the impression that the difference between the industrial organisation of Yorkshire and the West of England was fundamental, this was not so.[16]

But surely it was indeed so, as Heaton himself seems to admit!

> The typical clothier of the South Western counties, working on a large scale had become wealthy, and according to a pamphlet by May (A Declaration of the State of Clothing now used within the Realm, 1613) increased in fame and riches, his house like a King's court, his table replenished with feasts, his hospitality bountiful, and with such plenty and content on every side that crowned heads were highly pleased with the entertainment received at his hands.

Certainly there were differences in size between clothiers in the two areas, but the important point is that there was nothing in the West Riding to compare with the unified body of well-to-do clothiers, operating in the trade in a large way, that existed in the West. There were no large families dominating the trade, such as the Longs of Wraxall, the Hortons of Westwood and the Stumps of Malmesbury.

There was, Heaton goes on to say, one feature common to all, the close alliance between farming and industry. But this connection was much stronger in Yorkshire than in the West. The major West-country clothiers were not farmers, although they may have later

21

used the money they made in clothing to become landowners.

One of the most interesting facets of the West Riding woollen trade of the sixteenth century was the Halifax Act of 1555[17], whereby in view of local conditions, Halifax was given special permission to purchase wool through middlemen whilst the rest of the country was forbidden to do so. Too much should not be made of this special permission as the Act forbidding middlemen to deal in wool never operated efficiently in any part of the country; in so far as it proves anything at all, it proves the smallness of the Halifax clothiers.

Another interesting question relates to apprenticeship and the extent to which the laws were obeyed. Apprenticeship was probably regarded inside the clothing areas more as a matter of industrial convenience than as one involving any legal compulsion. The Government also made many attempts to regulate wages: the justices were given instructions to rate the wages of any labourers, weavers and workmen or workwomen whatsoever, whether working by the day, week, month, year, or taking work at any person's hands to be done at home. These assessments were intended to state a minimum wage for the textile workers, and any clothier who refused to pay as large a wage to his weavers as should be ordained in this assessment was to be fined 10s for each offence. These wage regulations did the workers some good. Those not covered by them, notably the spinners, were particularly badly paid, 2d to 4d a day being reckoned as normal earnings. Considering the shortage of yarn it is a mystery that hand spinners were so poorly rewarded. The real wages paid to all textile workers declined during the Tudor period; in monetary terms they remained stationary but there was a considerable increase in general prices.

Another side of the Tudor cloth trade relates to the increasing number of complaints regarding bad cloth. But in fact Yorkshire cloths had not deteriorated; rather had they improved, and, because they had improved and demanded a national and international market, complaints occasionally came into the news. The antiquarian Fuller writes in an often-quoted passage:

> As I am glad to hear of the plenty of a coarser kind of cloth made in this County, at Halifax, Leeds and elsewhere, whereby the meaner sort are much employed and the middle sort enriched; so I am sorry for

the general complaints made thereof in so much as it has become a general bye-word 'to shrink as northern cloths' (a giant to the eye and a dwarf in the use thereof) to signify such as fail their friends in deepest needs depending on their assistance. Sad that the sheep, the emblem of innocence, should unwittingly cover so much craft under the wool thereof; and sadder that fullers commended in scripture for making cloths white should justly be condemned for making their consciences black by such fraudulent practices.

A pretty piece of prose but, as far as the Yorkshire woollen trade is concerned, nonsense.

A brief study of the cloth trade in the Tudor period leads almost to amazement at the amount of legislation which the trade survived. What, for example, is one to make of the Act of 1597, whose main purpose was to do away with tenters, for how was cloth-making to continue unless the fabric was dried? The Government's continual worry about over-stretching reached ridiculous heights. Despite all these regulations, and despite the fact that it was still so much the poorer cousin of the Westcountry trade, the Yorkshire woollen industry did, during the sixteenth century, continue to expand its exports. John Crabtree of Halifax, who as keeper of the seal of cloths had special facilities for knowing the trade, said in 1638 that of the 80,000 kerseys manufactured in the West Riding 60,000 went abroad from the ports of London, Hull, York, Chester and Newcastle. Considering the simple beginnings and the comparative coarseness of the cloth made this was no mean achievement.

Many Tudor regulations had important effects later, and were the basis of the exciting events of the years around 1800. These old restrictions were then swept away in 1813, those concerning apprenticeship in 1814. It is interesting to recall that the Speaker in the House of Commons at that time saw fit to comment that 'the reign of Elizabeth, though glorious, was not one in which sound principles of commerce were known'.

THE STUART PERIOD

Although the seventeenth century, particularly the second half, was in the West Riding of Yorkshire a period of some progress and of a certain increase in the types of cloth made, all still agreed that the Yorkshire fabrics were inferior in quality to those of both the

West of England and East Anglia. It was said that although the wools of Lincolnshire and Leicester used by the Yorkshire clothier were as fine as the wools favoured by the West of England, yet the difference remained. When the clothiers of the West of England and East Anglia used the same wools as Yorkshire, the cloths which they made sold at 12s (60p), £1, even as high as 26s (£1.30) a yard, compared with 3s (15p) and 4s (20p) if made in Yorkshire. This difference in price was probably due to the fact that Yorkshire still made narrow-width cloths whilst the West of England made broadcloth, and to the fact that the wool may well have been taken from different parts of the same sheep. Indeed one writer stressed the importance of sorting: 'He conceived a good sorting of wools in the southern parts as the reason why the clothiers in the southern parts do make their cloths finer and of greater value by much than the northern kerseys, although the wool be alike in fineness from the sheep'.[18]

Kerseys continued to be made because they were cheap. Most of the wool used in them would have been grown locally, but from the evidence given in a 1638 lawsuit, it does seem that a certain amount of wool was obtained from other areas such as Lincolnshire and Leicestershire, though it was probably still the coarser, poorer type. Any fine wool available was bought by those areas making the more expensive cloths.

During the seventeenth century the West of England clothiers, in their attempt to replace the trade they had lost through Alderman Cockayne's unfortunate experiment[19], turned to making lighter-weight and finer cloth. One of the problems they met was the difficulty of obtaining sufficient fine wool. English wool was already deteriorating in quality and the more progressive West of England clothiers turned increasingly to Spanish wool, the true Merino, which was certainly far better than anything that was being grown or had ever been grown in Britain. At this comparatively early period Yorkshire did not use it. In fact for the first half of the seventeenth century, Yorkshire as well as the West of England showed signs of a comparative stagnation in the woollen industry. Yorkshire was not as badly damaged by Cockayne's experiment as was the Westcountry, but this experiment was only one example of the difficulties facing the wool-textile trade at the time.

Trade was often bad, and this led to the usual Government action : the justices of the peace for the West Riding and those of the Westcountry were to call the clothiers before them in order to select two representatives who should be able to place before the commissioners the grievances of the county from which they came. The commissioners were kept busy with complaints, for example that too few people in England wore good woollen cloth and were instead buying too many silk and foreign stuffs. This, it was pointed out, over-balanced British trade, was bad for all, and should be stopped. Then again it was said that the policy of Colbert in France had succeeded in establishing an active, prosperous textile industry which was challenging our own traditional markets and, as a result, gentlemen in Poland who had previously clothed their attendants with English cloth were now buying elsewhere. All this has a familiar ring; it was to some extent true, because foreign trade did not increase. The Yorkshire export trade was coming more under the influence of the Merchant Adventurers, but this body never dominated conditions there to the extent they did in the West of England.

The early Stuart Governments attempted to increase state control over industry in general, mainly for financial reasons, and the new regulations were applied to the woollen trade as to all other sections of the economic community. Cloth was an excellent commodity to tax, and the Government was determined that no section of the trade should escape—the cloths of the West Riding must bear their share like all the others. There were, of course, no lack of laws on the statute book stipulating what each clothier should pay.

Complaints continued to be made, mainly by the London merchants and factors, about the ill-use of tenters, which it was said should only be set up in open places. One is reminded of the guild restrictions that weaving should only be done in lower rooms where the workmen could be seen. Great emphasis was placed on the width and length of cloths when fully wetted and shrunk, and the weight was to be that of pieces when thoroughly cleaned and dried. No cloth was to be stretched in tentering more than 1 yd in length, or $\frac{1}{4}$ yd in breadth.

The Government's approach to the problem of regulating the wool-textile trade in the West Riding culminated in the Yorkshire Wool Trial of 1613 when many witnesses, some of considerable age, were brought from different parts of the county to give evidence.[20] Just as the aulnage accounts throw some light on conditions during medieval times, so the details of the great trials in the Court of the Exchequer give a picture of the Yorkshire woollen trade in the seventeenth century. Kerseys, if they measured less than half a cloth of assize, had in the early days of the trade been exempt from taxation; but from the passing of the Statute of 17 Richard II until 1601, 1d a cloth was paid as aulnage and subsidy. The Duke of Lennox was given the office of Aulnager of the old Draperies of the county and for the next fourteen years the Duke's attempt to obtain an increased fee and the North-country clothiers' resistance was fought out in the courts.

The administrative machinery of the aulnager's office at that time was somewhat involved. Though the Duke held the patent from the Crown he had farmed out the office to Sir Thomas Vavasour, Sir John Watts and Sir John Middleton, who in their turn had employed two deputy aulnagers, George Dixon and Tom Sindall. In addition, there were the searchers who reported any deficiency in the cloth that it suited them to discover; but they owed no allegiance to the aulnagers, being appointed by the local magistrates. The Attorney General's complaint was that gradually kerseys had increased in length from 12 to 24 yd, and proportionately in weight, yet still the clothiers continued to pay the same aulnage and subsidy. They refused to pay 1½d which the aulnagers considered was the correct amount.

Much miscellaneous information concerning the trade was given in the bill of complaint and in the evidence of the witnesses. Richard Law, one of the defending clothiers, declared that at least 20,000 men, women and children were employed in making kerseys in the four parishes of Halifax, Bradford, Bingley and Keighley. The defendants dealt with special pride on what seem irrelevant matters, such as the huge expenditure on the old and poor (£40 a month in Halifax alone), their generosity in keeping ten preachers, their success in eliminating the popish recusants—'Not one in the whole parish'; and by a somewhat curious process of reasoning, all these virtues were attributed to the making of the said northern kerseys.

The clothiers won the day:

It appeared to this court that it hath been heretofore used and accustomed of very long and ancient time without any interruption, until now of late that the clothiers inhabiting within the parishes of Halifax, Bradford, Bingley and Keighley have only paid the sum or rate of 1d for subsidy and aulnage of each kersey and no more. And that the same hath been during all the said time accepted as the proper and one sum payable for the subsidy and aulnage of a kersey as this court now conceiveth, and therefore without great and just cause being shown to the contrary the court thought it not fit to be altered.

There was another trial before the Court of Exchequer in 1637. The cloth trade had certainly developed during the twenty-four years between the trials; the parish of Halifax was said to have 12,000 textile workers, and Bradford, Bingley and Keighley 10,000. The bill of complaint of the Halifax men and the defendants' answers followed the lines of the case tried in 1613. References were made to the godliness of the makers of kerseys and their charity to the poor; their efforts on behalf of true religion were eloquently described. The deputy aulnager was said to be disqualified because he was an unskilled maker of cloth, and because his aged father kept a tippling house and was a man of mean quality and small estate. The clothiers complained that the tax agents had again begun to demand 1½d instead of 1d for subsidy and aulnage. They stated that before this extortion began, about £6,000 per year was paid into the customs from the said four parishes of Halifax, Bradford, Bingley and Keighley, but they took a doleful view of the future if these extortions continued. They further argued that the fact that the exaction would fall on people entirely unable to bear any additional burdens increased the wickedness of the proceedings, and pleaded that the places they inhabited were so mountainous and rough, and so barren and unfruitful, that they did not yield victuals for a third part of the inhabitants, and the poor that spun the wool there, though they worked very hard, could not even earn 4d a day. This dismal picture was painted in even darker colours by the evidence of many witnesses, one of whom considered that no spinner could ordinarily addle (earn) above 3d or 4d a day. Another said that only the strongest could earn 4d, the majority earned 2d or 3d, while the daily maximum wage of the spinner in the Keighley district was stated to be 3d; and most spinners earned 2d.

The amount of money demanded was not the only ground for the complaint. It was stated that the aulnager's agent, contrary to custom, refused to visit outlying country districts where people wished their cloths to be sealed and the clothiers had to fetch the seal themselves—agents were exacting more money and doing less work.

There is unfortunately no definite information as to the verdict in this second trial. We know however that at a still later trial in 1676 two people who had been witnesses at the earlier suit, recollecting what had happened forty years before, said the then aulnager, after he had spent a great deal of money, desisted the suit and accepted 1d for each seal.

The seventeenth century saw the beginning of selling at the cloth markets which were to play so large a part in the development of the woollen trade in Yorkshire in the eighteenth century, but the whole question of their growth and development is better described in the next section dealing with the time when Defoe's classic account was written.

There were few major technical changes during the seventeenth century and, as regards the type of cloths made, there was no change in Yorkshire equal to that in the Westcountry where the old undyed white broadcloth was replaced by the lighter-weight coloured broadcloth. It was of course this type of lighter broadcloth which the leading Yorkshire clothiers in the next century were to copy and in the end produce efficiently, but as yet their trade was mainly confined to kerseys. Nor is there any real sign that the Yorkshire trade was affected by the growth of the new draperies in East Anglia. The latter and the closely allied serges of the Somerset-Devon borders in the extreme south-west represented the real growth-section of the wool-textile industry in the seventeenth century.

Taken as a whole, therefore, the seventeenth century in Yorkshire was a comparatively uninteresting period, a preface as it were to the great days of the eighteenth century, when Yorkshire assumed the place it has never lost as the great wool-cloth-making centre of the world. Not only was her woollen trade to surpass in importance the traditional industry of the West of England, but even more important the worsted trade began, grew and finally took over completely the long-established Norwich trade.

THE EIGHTEENTH CENTURY

The eighteenth century was, in many ways, the most interesting in the development of the textile trade in Yorkshire. Fortunately we have Defoe's classic account. He found Halifax and Leeds were the great centres. Today one would tend to put Bradford and Huddersfield first, but in Defoe's time Bradford's great increase in population and her move to being the leading worsted centre in the world was only just beginning; she was still a small town and the development that was to lead to the lines 'On Bradford likewise look thou down, Where Satan keeps his seat'[21] had not begun.

In addition to the kerseys, still the main branch of the trade, the eighteenth century was the time of Yorkshire's successful attempt to turn to the better-quality broadcloths, and the output of these trebled between 1727 and 1770. The increase then became even more rapid, and by 1785 the area was producing six times as many broadcloths as it had done in 1727. In almost all fields Yorkshire's woollen cloths were rivalling, even supplanting, those from the West of England, and this change was taking place long before any machinery had been introduced into the trade. It is a mistake to see the coming of pre-eminence to Yorkshire in woollen manufacturing as having anything to do with what is commonly called the Industrial Revolution.

In 1772[22], Britain's total textile exports, including cotton, silk, etc, came to £4,500,000 and of this total Yorkshire was responsible for at least £2,300,000; in other words she so dominated the textile scene as to account for over half of the country's entire export trade in textiles. She was at this time the chief English textile centre, even more important than Lancashire, which was shortly to take the supreme place from her. As far as the woollen and worsted trades were concerned, however, Yorkshire was to go from strength to strength and it is in the period of what one would like to call her youth, in the eighteenth century, that the seeds of her greatness lay. This vast expansion took place in what was essentially a domestic industry, there were no factories of any importance. It has been stated that a few existed—Professor Heaton says scarcely twenty as late as 1800—but they were quite unimportant early in the eighteenth century, and throughout it no one thought of using power looms for woollen cloths. The latter were not used before 1820 and as late as 1850 half the woollen workers were said to be outside the factory system.

It is therefore abundantly clear that in the eighteenth century the Yorkshire woollen, and to a lesser extent the early worsted, trades were basically domestic, non-factory industries. As regards the first mentioned, there can be few cases in history where a traditional industry, an industry which has not been fertilised by some new invention, has suddenly progressed at such a rate; even today it remains difficult to understand why it happened. Although similar in some respects, the rise of the worsted trade followed rather different lines. There were, for example, no cloth halls; later eighteenth-century inventions were to have more important effects on worsted than on woollen manufacture; there was also the major difference that worsted was not a traditional industry and therefore one might reasonably expect a more rapid growth. The interesting fact is that the eighteenth century was such a period of expansion in both branches; it was this that gave the whole picture of industrial life in Yorkshire such vigour.

The Woollen Trade

Cloth Halls and Merchants

The two major themes in the growth of the Yorkshire woollen trade during the eighteenth century were, firstly, the rise of the cloth halls and, secondly, the increased prominence of the merchants. The cloth halls were a direct growth from Defoe's market on the bridge (see Appendix One). As the trade increased some other centre for selling was clearly needed; consequently the cloth halls were built, reproducing exactly the features Defoe saw. Each clothier had a stall, the merchants made their purchases as before, and the halls were the centre of the woollen trade until the end of the century—their remains still provide an interesting section of Yorkshire's industrial architecture.[23] At first all merchants bought their cloths from the clothiers at the cloth halls; later those whose businesses expanded and became more prosperous bypassed the halls and gave large orders direct for goods to be made according to sample and definite specification. But through the century the cloth halls continued to play a large part in the trade. Defoe's account from the early part of the century, when the selling took place in the streets, is supplemented by that of Baines who, although writing at a much later period, gives a picture which represents the long-established position. Among much that was changing this method of selling remained, and it gives a remarkable unity to the eighteenth-century woollen trade in Yorkshire: although the trade was expanding much faster than that of the West of England, the separation between master-clothier and worker noticeable in Wiltshire and Gloucester is much less evident.

The second theme, the increased prominence of the merchants, was very important. The merchants were responsible for much of the growth of the trade, and if one had to single out the most significant difference between the Yorkshire and the West of England industries particularly as regards their relative growths, one would pinpoint these merchants. Later during the early years of the nineteenth century, they were a major force behind factory development.

The merchants occupied something of the place in the Yorkshire trade of the large so-called 'gentlemen clothiers' in the West of England. But unlike the West of England clothiers they looked to the future, and were the forerunners of growth, not the organisers of an old-fashioned industry. These Yorkshire merchants were more enterprising and more inclined to go out and see what the customers wanted than were the clothiers of the South West—they were newcomers and had initiative.

One of the first signs that the merchants were developing new ideas was shown in their increased tendency to establish their own finishing shops. In Yorkshire the domestic clothier usually attended to the fulling himself and, if he supplied cloth to the coloured-cloth halls, he also did the dyeing. In the case of the white-cloth hall, however, the cloths were only fulled by the clothiers and the merchants did the cloth-working in their own establishments, or had it done for them in independent finishing shops working on a commission basis. These establishments were the forerunners of the factories of the future, although they did not in the eighteenth century use any power-driven machinery. The merchants who bought coloured cloths, that is those that had been finished, did not play this distinctive part in the industry's story.

Technical Changes

Until the end of the eighteenth century important technical changes were mainly confined to the yarn-producing side of the trade. Arkwright developed Paul's idea of roller-spinning into a brilliant new conception used first for cotton and then for worsted, but never for woollen yarn. On the other hand the jenny invented by Hargreaves was primarily a machine for spinning all types of woollen yarn. The early jennies were small and used in the cottages, and fitted well into the domestic system as practised in Yorkshire.

The position was different with the processes before the actual spinning. Lewis Paul of roller-spinning fame and a Leominster manufacturer named Bourn had, in the same year, invented the principle of rotary carding.[24] Bourn's idea came first and was the better, and gradually the Lancashire cotton trade took it up. From there it passed to Yorkshire and by the end of the eighteenth century a large part of the scribbling and carding was done by machine —card wire previously fitted to hand cards was placed around rollers, which were usually driven by water power. In the West of England scribbling mills were usually combined with fulling mills, but in Yorkshire the position was somewhat different. Fulling mills in the sense that they were known in the West were not common, and the more usual practice was to erect new buildings to undertake the scribbling and carding.

The small domestic clothiers came to realise that yarn must be at least partly machine-spun if they were to keep their looms running; they therefore usually combined to finance the erection of a small scribbling mill on a more or less co-operative basis and had their raw material processed there. This important stage of factory building came at about the same time as the merchants established finishing shops, but as it was done by the small domestic clothiers for their own benefit it brought none of the hatred of the factories that was later to arise. There are few better accounts of spinning in those days than that given by Joseph Lawson in *Progress in Pudsey* (see Appendix Two).

The Domestic System

Defoe has given a fine picture of the trade, but it is a pity that he did not tell us a little more about the clothiers' homes that were scattered in the valleys of the West Riding. If one could see them as they were, possibly the most noticeable thing would be the large numbers of tenter frames which, stretching on the sloping ground at the side of the clothing hamlets, might indeed be compared with the advertisement hoardings so well-known outside cities today. Tenter frames can still sometimes be seen near textile centres in Southern Europe; they must have been far more common in eighteenth-century Yorkshire.

In these valley homes the domestic clothier himself, working usually with his wife and family, and occasionally with the help of one or maybe two apprentices and perhaps a journeyman, continued much as he had done for centuries. Owing to the great expansion of the Yorkshire trade he was more prosperous than ever before. Indeed an almost Arcadian conception of eighteenth-century life has been painted, though it has been challenged; Professor Heaton never accepted it, but he has perhaps gone too far the other way. There can be no doubt that the 'good old days' of the eighteenth century remained a very conscious memory in Yorkshire, and although one must almost always view such nostalgia with considerable caution, yet there was a real basis for this tradition. The days when one lived in one's own home and combined the weaving and other sides of cloth-making with a certain amount of farming did, in the grim days of the early nineteenth century, appear as a happiness which had been lost. Southey spoke of 'contentment spinning at the cottage door', a view which was definitely held by the workers themselves. James in his *History and Topography of Bradford* states, on the authority of an old villager, that the women and children of the dales would go out on a sunny day with their spinning wheels to some particularly pleasant spot to work. As far as Yorkshire's many wet days were concerned, when work would have to be crowded indoors, James himself comments, 'These spinners in the sun were not free from the vice imputed to their grand-daughters at the modern tea table'.

33

C

The 1806 Parliamentary Report makes quite clear that the conservatism of the domestic workers was based upon a very real understanding of what factory life was like. J. L. Hammond, who based his views on this report, was surely right when he too said that those who look back from a vantage point in the twentieth century, with their knowledge of the increased wealth the factory system brought, should not ignore the strongly expressed views of the hand-loom weavers and other textile workers. Those responsible for the 1806 Report were sympathetic to the Yorkshire workers. They hated the growth of unions which they discovered among the latter, but that is another story, and few writers have stated the position of the domestic clothiers as well as they did in their summary:[25]

> Hand-loom work in the weaver's own cottage gratifies that innate comfort and independence which all more or less feel, by leaving the workman entirely the master of his own time and sole guide of his actions. He can play or idle as feeling and inclination lead him; rise early or late and apply himself as assiduously or carelessly as he pleases and work at any time by increased exertions hours previously sacrificed to indulgence or recreation. There is scarcely another condition of any of our working population thus free of external authority.

The Report actually stresses the advantage of the domestic system in the minds of those who gave evidence, for example:

> Certainly we prefer having work in our own homes. We can begin sooner or later and do as we like in that respect, and those of us who have families have an opportunity in one way or another of training them up in some little business.

Compared with the life of most work-people at the time it was not a bad life. Some writers have had much to say of the long hours worked for a mere pittance by these domestic hand-loom weavers, and the fact that they worked their children hard. Children were indeed a valuable source of labour to these small clothiers; if they had none they had to employ journeymen or apprentices. But child labour in the domestic system was not normally comparable to child labour in the harsh conditions of the early factories, although an exception should be made where weavers employed parish apprentices. Parents have usually been fond of their children and would rarely have ill-used them or worked them the long hours demanded by the overseers in the early factories. There was a world of difference between a child of five to seven spinning at his own cottage door with his parents—more important perhaps his own brothers and sisters—around him, the Yorkshire countryside coming down to his very feet, and a child working twelve or more hours a day in a factory.

As we have seen, the Yorkshire domestic system responded admirably to the sudden expansion of the market. Economic historians sometimes overstress the advantages of large-scale production; even with our modern scientific machines these advantages are occasionally over-emphasised. In the early factories there was little advantage in scale; in the eighteenth century there was none at all. The economist tends to forget how hardworking and efficient a small family unit could be. He deplores the weekly journey to the cloth hall, but forgets that when the factory was in the same town as the cloth hall the worker had to make the journey every day. The assumption seems to be that in the former case there was a waste of time, the journey coming out of what should have been the working day, but in terms of human effort and happiness there was no real difference; far better make the journey only once or twice a week than daily. Enough has not been made of the great waste of time from travelling to work during the early days of the factory system—dwellings were often two hours away from the factories and these long walks certainly lingered in the memory.

The Worsted Trade

Surpassing in importance the great growth in the woollen trade, the coming of the worsted trade to Yorkshire from other areas of the country was one of the outstanding events in the industrial history of England, and certainly of supreme importance to Yorkshire itself. There are many reasons for making this statement. Without doubt, the future greatness of the Yorkshire textile trade depended upon it, not only as regards the worsted trade itself but also to some extent the woollen. It was the presence of the prosperous worsted trade, providing as it did the raw material for new types of waste, that did much to foster the growth of the low woollen trade in the nineteenth century.

Yorkshire remained a major producer of woollen cloths and

obtained the lead over the West of England because she turned to these cheaper woollen fabrics. One should also always remember that although by the end of the eighteenth century Yorkshire had successfully challenged the West of England in broadcloth manufacture, yet both areas were to find traditional goods largely replaced by the new worsted fabrics.

The words woollen and worsted cause much confusion to those not in the trade—they are indeed rather foolish. Both woollen and worsted cloths are made from wool, and together they form the two sections of the wool industry of the world. People outside the industry rarely realise how completely these two sections of the trade differed in the past and still differ today; they have always been and still remain two separate industries. The basic differences are fundamental and four in number.

Firstly, worsteds are made from long wool, woollens from short wools; secondly, in preparing the wool for spinning, that for worsteds is combed whereas that for woollens is carded; thirdly, yarn spun from woollen sliver is drafted, ie drawn out, while the twist is inserted, whereas that for worsteds is drafted without twist, this being put in afterwards. Finally, cloths made from woollen yarns are fulled, those from worsted are not. It will be noticed that of these four major differences one relates to the raw material used, two to the manufacture of the yarn, and one to the finishing. There were no fundamental differences in weaving.

The first difference is the most important and is the one upon which all the others ultimately depend. Long wool is chosen for worsteds because it is going to be combed (combing removes any short fibres), and it is spun without twist; finally, because the long wool has produced stronger yarn, fulling, which strengthens the fabric, is omitted. Short wool cannot be combed and cannot be spun without twist; only by fulling is a strong cloth obtained from it.

When spinning wheels were developed these differences were accentuated. Woollens were spun on the big wheel, worsteds on the Jersey or Saxony wheel with flyer mechanism attached, but the basic difference leading to the development of the two separate techniques still came from the fact that the woollens were made from short and the worsteds from long wools, each requiring a different twisting process. Exactly the same distinction continued when spinning was mechanised, and was made even sharper by the fact that whereas carding was mechanised around 1750, combing was the last process to be successfully mechanised; this was not in fact done until the middle of the nineteenth century.

The Making of Worsteds

The sequence of processes in the worsted trade has always differed considerably from that in the woollen and, as the history of the worsted trade in Yorkshire was determined by these differences, it is convenient to consider here the way worsted cloths were made.

Because the worsted comber removes all short fibres, whereas the woollen carder attempts to keep fibres of all lengths in his yarn, the sorting of the fleece occupied a more important place in worsted-yarn manufacture than it did in woollen. Indeed today hardly any sorting is done in the woollen trade, whereas the process remains relatively important with worsteds. This distinction was not so absolute in the eighteenth century, but the worsted sorter would always have been more concerned than the woollen to see that the shorter wools were not included in the batches that he sent forward to be combed. Combing is, and always has been, a key process in the manufacture of worsted fabrics; indeed the history of worsted manufacturing cannot be understood without appreciating exactly what it involved. Hand combing has a history stretching back for many hundreds of years, and we have accurate accounts of how it was done during the later days of its history. The earliest known references come from the Sumerian civilisation of about 1500 BC but nothing is known of the methods used. Many centuries later a French painting showed the martyrdom of St Blaise, and the combs with which he was being tortured resemble those that were in use before the introduction of machine combing. St Blaise, although destined to become the patron saint of the combers, had himself no connection with textiles; the combs with which he actually suffered martyrdom were in fact not those specifically used by the combers, although later paintings usually show them as such.

There are many descriptions of hand combing and several writers have given versions which are not always entirely accurate. Fortunately A. H. Ling Roth, curator of the Bankfield Museum of

Halifax, many years ago had a visit from an old man who told him that he had been a hand comber in his youth. Ling Roth persuaded his visitor to carry out the process, took pictures of it, and published an excellent pamphlet entitled *Hand Combing*. The combs consisted of two or three rows of long, tapering steel teeth set in a wooden handle. Before being used they were heated over a fire; a stove is always shown in any picture of the process. One comb was then fixed to a hook on a post. The scoured wool was oiled with olive oil or butter, and then about 2 lb of wool was fixed to the teeth of the comb on the post and worked with the other. Combing continued until the wool had all passed to the second comb, when the process was repeated. When combing was completed the wool was taken off in a long sliver and rolled into a top; the short noils remained on the comb.

The point about combing that was to affect the future geographical distribution of the industry was that it was a guild occupation. As we have seen, none of the processes involved in yarn-making on the woollen principle were ever organised as a guild—we never hear of a guild of carders or a guild of spinners, presumably because these processes were normally done by women. The combers' guild was well organised, and the wool combers travelled about the country to wherever there was wool to be combed, which later made the transition of the industry from East Anglia to Yorkshire comparatively easy.

The conversion of the combed top to yarn was originally done with distaff and spindle and continued to be so, even after the invention of the simple spinning wheel. Because the short fibres had been removed worsted top could be drafted without the addition of twist; consequently the idea of spindle-drafting with twist, which was brought to its full technical development with the simple spinning wheel, produced no advantage. These first wheels consisted simply of a wooden wheel driving a spindle by means of a piece of string. The material to be spun was still carried on the distaff, the spinner drawing her fibres from this, but the drafting method changed. As she needed one hand to turn the wheel, she could not draw the fibres between the fingers of her two hands, so drafted between the tip of the spindle and the fingers of the other hand. During drafting she inserted whatever twist she needed by means of the wheel. When drafting was finished she inserted the remaining twist by revolving the wheel faster. Finally, when the length of yarn was spun, she moved the position of her thread relative to the spindle, and by again turning the wheel wound the yarn on to the spindle.[26]

Credit for the next invention is usually given to Johann Jurgen, a German woodcarver, and the piece of apparatus he introduced is still used, and known as the flyer. In 1530 he combined the flyer with the spindle and by means of it inserted the twist and wound the yarn on to a bobbin on the spindle at the same time. He deserves every credit for this invention, which as far as he was concerned was entirely original. The same principle was later used by Arkwright on his water frame, so it persists in one form of worsted spinning today. The idea however had been thought out and designed several years before by the great Renaissance genius Leonardo da Vinci. Leonardo died in 1519, so there can be no doubt he came first, but it is reasonably certain that Jurgen had not seen his sketches because da Vinci had introduced a system for adjusting the position of the winding-on which Jurgen would surely have used if he had seen it.

The Saxony wheel fitted with a treadle came into widespread use in the seventeenth and eighteenth centuries. This, by enabling the spinner to use both hands for controlling the drafting and thereby making twisting and winding continuous, led to a near approach to the full worsted process. There was no benefit as far as woollen spinning was concerned, but for worsteds it was a major advance. It is essential to appreciate just how important was the new method of spinning—it was the first of several technical developments that led to the great advance in worsted-yarn manufacture as compared to woollen. For a time, difficulties in developing machine combing prevented the worsted trade taking full advantage of new spinning methods but when, in the nineteenth century, combing was satisfactorily mechanised, the way was clear.

The mechanisation of spinning thus developed on two quite different lines, both springing from the two types of hand wheel: the Saxony wheel which gave continuous spinning and was ideally adapted for worsteds, and the simple wheel which gave discontinuous spinning and was best for short wools. The mechanisation of the first however was based on an entirely new concept, roller spinning, in which the drawing out of the sliver was done by a series of rollers revolving at different surface speeds. On the other hand, the second approach, Hargreaves' jenny, was an attempt to copy the action of spindle drafting upon the simple wheel in something approaching a mechanised form. The woollen fibres were drafted between one pair of rollers and a revolving spindle which inserted twist while the drawing out was taking place; it was not in any way as revolutionary an approach as roller drafting. It is strange that these two methods of machine spinning should have fitted so neatly into the two branches of the wool-textile trade, when one remembers that both were invented and developed mainly for cotton.

It is important to stress the differences between continuous and intermittent spinning, which the two eighteenth-century inventions confirmed and further defined. Roller spinning was continuous; there was no need to deliver a length of slubbing then stop and draw it, twist it and finally wind it on to a container. Given two pairs of rollers working at different surface speeds, and suitable material, the drawing took place continuously. As the yarn left the last pair of rollers, the twist was put in and the winding-on accomplished at the same time by means of the ingenious winding and twisting apparatus used by Jurgen, which these early inventors took over as it already existed.

The idea of roller drafting was the most sensational development ever introduced in the textile trade. It has proved to be the basis of most modern spinning systems, and is probably destined to supersede all others. As far as the worsted trade was concerned it was, in addition, adapted for the processes between carding and spinning, and today the drawing out of the top to the final thread in worsteds is entirely done by rollers.

There has been a great deal of discussion as to who was really responsible for the first original idea, but it has now been firmly established that Lewis Paul, whose carding invention has already been mentioned (p 32), was the brain behind it. He stands out as one of the most original minds in the textile trade. The original patent of 1738 was taken out in his name, and Wyatt, whom many people have tried to claim as the original inventor, appeared only as a witness. The original specification[27] was not very clear, but it is certain that several pairs of rollers were used and that each pair revolved faster than the previous one. This was the all-important feature that Paul invented.

Three points stand out as regards the patent: first, the brilliant idea is contained in its first part; secondly, the inventor only complicated this idea by suggesting that the rollers could give twist as well. Any attempt to introduce twist in this way would make roller drafting impossible, and Paul's failure to produce a practical machine probably came from his failure to see this. Thirdly, the last part of his patent has nothing to do with the first, and is really only a form of spindle drafting, which Paul complicated by presumably attempting to wind the yarn simultaneously. This is clearly impossible; twisting and winding with the help of the flyer can be done simultaneously, but not drafting and winding. The idea was not widely adopted—far from it; the original inventor obviously had not properly developed it. Indeed Paul, in a specification for another patent twenty years later, abandoned the roller idea and turned to the alternative method of drafting between the spindle point and a pair of rollers. Undoubtedly he had given up hope of making a successful practical machine of his first idea.[28]

After Paul and Wyatt's idea failed we know surprisingly little about events except that slowly the knowledge of what had been done reached Lancashire and that several people there attempted to succeed in the idea of roller spinning. It seems that much of this knowledge came via a mill that Daniel Bourn, the inventor of the rotary carding machine, set up at Leominster. This mill was partly owned by men from Lancashire, which would have allowed information on these new discoveries to reach the rapidly expanding cotton trade. At any rate close connection between Yorkshire and Lancashire must have helped Yorkshire to take up these ideas before they could reach East Anglia. Bourn's mill was burnt down in 1754 and was not rebuilt, but by this time experiments had already started in Lancashire with a circular carding machine, although not as yet with the roller-spinning idea.

It was left to Richard Arkwright to bring the idea of roller spinning, which had been so widely discussed during the years following Paul and Wyatt's original patent, to a successful conclusion. Obviously he was not the originator of the idea, and he doubtlessly profited by what had already been done in Lancashire, but this hardly lessens the importance of what he did towards making a successful machine.

Before Arkwright revolutionised cotton spinning—and indirectly worsted spinning as well—the raw material, after opening and cleaning, was still usually carded by hand. The slubbing was drawn out of it and slightly twisted on the spinning wheel to make a roving, which was again spun on a wheel. Arkwright's final success in producing a successful spinning machine swept all this away, and it was due to him far more than to anybody else that the spinning factory became a practical proposition. Sir Edward Baines himself, in his *History of the Cotton Manufacture in Great Britain*, published in 1835, referred to Arkwright's unrivalled sagacity in estimating at their true value the mechanical contrivances of others.

It has been truly said that Arkwright was the chief architect of the cotton industry, and he did the same for worsted manufacture. The more one studies him the more he appears to be the epitome of the famous cotton trade he made possible. There is the same determination to work hard and long that made cotton one of the main foundations of Britain's nineteenth-century industrial power; but it was combined, one must admit, with a certain narrowness which was perhaps the great fault of the whole period.

The development of roller spinning, although originally planned for the cotton trade, has been treated in detail because the main reason for the great progress made by worsted manufacture in the late eighteenth and early nineteenth centuries lay in the fact that this sequence of processes developed by Arkwright admirably suited the spinning of long wool.

The Decline of East Anglian Worsteds

Meanwhile in East Anglia the worsted trade which had begun many centuries before—the tradition of course is that 'worsted' derives from a village of that name—continued to manufacture on old-established lines. There was no sign at all that the trade there realised that revolutionary developments were taking place which were to end traditional methods.

Combing, that crucial worsted process, was a skilled operation, and as mentioned earlier, was done by men who wandered throughout England and combed the wool where they found it; one is reminded in many ways of the shearers in Australia today. The fact that the key men in the trade moved about the country made it comparatively easy for the following processes, ie the actual spinning and weaving, to be done anywhere. Only the finishing, which as far as worsteds were concerned was comparatively simple, and the selling routine, remained to give Norfolk a real advantage over any other district.

Until the second half of the eighteenth century worsted manufacture remained relatively unimportant as compared with woollen. No one then could have imagined that during the next hundred years it was to become the main part of the industry.

It is easy to see now that East Anglia was not well placed to take advantage of the new opportunities presented by eighteenth-century inventions. There were many reasons, one being the fact that the rising population of Britain needed more foodstuffs including meat : mainly through the work of Bakewell this meant, as far as sheep were concerned, the breeding of larger animals which inevitably had longer wool suitable for combing, and these animals were in the North. More generally East Anglia, besides clinging to her traditional trading customs, lacked both water power and coal. Arkwright soon showed that the frame he had developed could be driven by water power—it was given the name 'water-frame'. Even if spinners in East Anglia had realised what was happening it would have been extremely difficult for them to have found sufficient or adequate water power to equip and drive spinning mills. There was also the fact that the industrial leaders there had become gentlemen and lacked the close connection with actual cloth-making which was so noticeable a feature of the Yorkshire scene. In addition the increase in the population of England was calling for increased quantities of relatively low-priced cloths. The Yorkshire worsted manufacturers made a plain cloth which was within the range of the less well to do classes, whereas Norfolk went on making expensive fabrics for which the demand was certainly not increasing. Finally, Yorkshire's nearness to Lancashire, as we have seen, gave her the opportunity of seizing on the new machine developments.

43

It is noticeable that the worsted trade tended to do best in those areas of the West Riding of Yorkshire which were nearest to the Lancashire cotton towns.

Several attempts have been made to date the beginning of the worsted trade in the West Riding, and the evidence suggests it began around the year 1700. Previously, long wools grown in the Yorkshire dales were combed by the guild combers during their travels, and the combed tops, or more likely the spun yarn, taken to Norfolk. Thus a kind of export trade had arisen which must have been a very real challenge to the enterprising men who were making the Yorkshire woollen trade the foremost in the country.

J. H. Clapham in his classic paper[29] seized upon the importance of the combers, and in this he was surely right:

> An interesting group connected with the Norwich trade and the worsted trade generally were the master combers. Your ordinary domestic spinner did not carry on the delicate task of combing. She had to receive combed tops from a specialist. So throughout the eighteenth century we find combing carried on all over the country. The masters were men of moderate substance, the journeymen supplied some of the earliest trade unions. There can, I think, be no doubt as to the part played by these master combers in connection with the import of yarn from other counties, which was one of the dangerous aspects of the Norwich industry.

Norfolk wool was never combed in the eighteenth century—it was too short. It mostly went to Yorkshire to be made into woollen cloth. Defoe found the Norwich men buying Lincoln long wool at Stourbridge Fair in 1723, and was told that they also imported many thousand packs of yarn from counties as far afield as Yorkshire and Westmorland. It is probable, from the very nature of the worsted processes and the known fact of forty years later, that the yarn-selling master comber had existed for some time in every district from which Norfolk drew her supplies early in the eighteenth century. The danger of the system to East Anglia is obvious.

Yorkshire excelled in two main types of worsted fabrics, in the production of which it was easiest to compete with Norwich—the plain simple worsteds of which the camlets used for raincoats before the days of Mr Mackintosh, and the shalloons worn by the female workingclass were typical. Yorkshire started her competition with the cheaper fabrics, and by about 1751 she was doing a large trade in plain worsteds; as yet the other areas making worsteds did not suffer, since the trade was expanding rapidly. But 1741 was only the beginning of Yorkshire competition. During the following years she made rapid progress and soon her goods supplied much of the home demand and some were exported. Next she began to experiment with finer cloth, and by 1772 the value of the worsteds made in the West Riding equalled those from Norwich and the surrounding districts.

If the outline is clear the details are confused. It is impossible to say who saw the great opportunity which existed but Halifax seems to have been the main centre of the first great period of development. Holroyd's correspondence shows that by 1706 bays were being made, and thirty years later Sam Hill was making bocking bays and experimenting with shalloons. In 1791 John Sutcliffe was making nothing but fine worsteds. All were Halifax clothiers and although it is difficult to discover who built up the worsted trade in the West Riding it was probably men of the type of Sam Hill. There had been many periods of depression in the woollen trade during the seventeenth century, and consequently more clothiers turned their attention to Norwich stuffs, shalloons and bays. Hill's correspondence shows the way in which he attempted to develop the trade in worsteds. It was a difficult job, and we find him writing in 1738: 'I am perfectly sick . . . no hope of the shalloon business'. But he went on experimenting, and a little later wrote: 'I think it is now very evident that these manufactures will come in spite of fate to these northern counties'.[30] How right he was! Miss Maud Sellers, author of the economic section of the *Victoria County History of Yorkshire*, wrote: 'Possibly a factor in bringing about this remarkable success was that from the outset the trade was organised on more or less capitalist lines'. Clapham thought the founders of the Yorkshire worsted trade were men of means, merchants perhaps or master combers.

The more adventurous of the many small capitalists engaged in the woollen trade would always have been looking for new cloths to make and would have been prepared to venture their hard-earned savings. Eighteenth-century writers stress this characteristic of the Yorkshire scene. The elimination of the two trading companies helped by clearing away out-of-date trading methods. Above all, the knowledge gained from centuries of handling wool produced a skill that could be adapted for worsteds. Although the expansion took place before the invention of machinery, the earlier development of the Jersey or Saxony wheel was a powerful influence and fitted in well with the increased supplies of long wool. Later, the increased strength of worsted yarn played its part in permitting other machinery to be used earlier than was the case with woollens. Generally, however, the factory system had nothing to do with the new trade development, and the first worsted mill is usually dated 1787. Although different in so many ways, the thriving young worsted trade can truly be considered another type of the all-embracing Yorkshire domestic system.

The local Halifax tradition is that the shalloons were introduced at the beginning of the 1700s, followed shortly after by figured fabrics. Throughout the eighteenth century Halifax remained the chief town with the clothiers well spread into Airedale and Calderdale, even across into Lancashire. After 1800, Bradford came more and more to dominate the worsted scene and Halifax's pre-eminence died with the French Wars.

INDUSTRIAL REVOLUTION IN THE WEST RIDING

The story of the Industrial Revolution in the West Riding of Yorkshire is complicated for many reasons. It must be remembered that the Industrial Revolution, particularly in its technical aspects, proceeded at quite different speeds in different parts of the country. Above all, the textile machines came to the West Riding much later than to Lancashire.

As we have seen, such machines depended on ideas originally developed for the cotton trade, and the pace at which such inventions could be adapted for the woollen and worsted trades differed considerably. For example, Arkwright's frame-spinning was well-suited to, and widely introduced into, worsted drawing and spinning by the end of the eighteenth century. On the other hand, the early cotton looms were not adaptable and hand weaving continued well into the nineteenth century. A continuous machine process for spinning was developed much earlier in the worsted than in the woollen trade, and equally important the hand loom had to be used for the weaker woollen yarn long after it had been supplanted by the power loom in the worsted trade. The modern and increasing dominance of the worsted section of the wool industry dates from the Industrial Revolution, although worsted-making existed much earlier in the domestic system. It is worth noting that complete continuity in woollen spinning has still not been obtained.

Early Machines and Riots

Much of the interest of this period comes from the attacks that the workers launched against these new machines. There had been few riots due to the coming of either spinning machines or the flying shuttle, although the question of whether the weavers had been apprenticed played a leading part in the disputes. The main struggle started to develop in 1802-3 and at first there was more concerted agitation in the West of England than in Yorkshire. These riots were organised by the cloth workers, and can only be understood in the context of the history of the development of the gig and shearing machines for finishing woollen and worsted cloths. This presented special problems, and the answers were found within the trade itself. There were two outstanding inventions: the first was the introduction of the circular milling machine, which replaced the fulling stocks; the second was the introduction of the shearing frame which replaced the old hand shears.

The circular milling machine was patented in 1833 by John Dyer of Trowbridge in Wiltshire. A controversy arose with Yorkshire as to who really invented it, but Dyer appears to have been the man. His milling machine closely resembled the one now in use, the only main difference being that he used three top rollers and a short spout.

The invention of the rotary cutting machine and the consequent departure of the old hand shears is a subject of more interest for several reasons, and it had considerable importance outside the field of its original intention—a circular cutting machine was seen in Stroud by a Mr Budding[31], and from it he produced the modern circular lawn mower; lawns previously had been cut with a scythe. The first idea in replacing the old hand shears was merely to put a number of shears into a frame and work them together. This possibility had occurred to Leonardo da Vinci but, as with his other textile ideas, nothing came of his sketch which was not known to the trade. It was not until 1784 that James Harmer of Sheffield placed several pairs of shears in a frame and operated them by means of a crank; he improved his device in 1794 and obtained several other patents. In some machines the shears travelled across the cloth, in others the cloth was drawn under them by means of rollers. These machines were used to some extent in France but never widely in England, partly one suspects because of the great opposition the machine shears evoked from the workers, and also because they were not really successful. It was the invention of the rotary machine that was technically crucial, and the first machine that definitely used this principle was made by an American, Samuel Dorr, and patented in England in 1794; but for some reason or other nothing more was heard of it. In America, however, machines based on it were produced and the machine reached France in 1812. In 1818, Collier, who already had a number of woollen and worsted patents to his credit, produced a circular machine, but it does not seem to have been very successful, and without much doubt the first real success for the rotary cutting machine in this country derived from a patent of James Lewis of Brimscombe, near Stroud, in 1815.

The machine is usually regarded as his own invention, and as having been made quite independently, but as drawings of the American model had been brought to England in 1811, Lewis may well have seen them. These early versions of a circular cutting machine differ in details but basically they were the same. The one important change was that, whereas in the earlier machines the cutting blade worked from list to list, later the circular blade was made the same width as the cloth, which passed through the machine in a lengthwise direction. Once the circular machine was working the days of hand shearing were finished, and this was in fact the case by 1830.

The 1802-3 riots, the legal struggle that followed in Parliament, and subsequent disturbances, form one of the most interesting of all aspects of the history of the Yorkshire woollen industry. There is no better starting point than the account given in the introduction to *The Report from the Select Committee appointed to Consider the*

State of the Woollen Manufacture in England, published by Parliament in 1806:

In July 1802 considerable riots and outrages took place in Wiltshire and Somerset, in consequence of an attempt by some of the master clothiers of those counties to set up a machine for dressing cloth called a gig mill. This machine was from various causes obnoxious to the workmen, and from an apprehension it is supposed of the disturbances which the first introduction of it produced it had never been set up in the above counties, although it had been for many years in use in Gloucestershire as well as in other parts; it had even been by no means unusual for the clothiers of Wiltshire and of some other districts where it was not worked to send their cloths a distance to be dressed by it. The disturbances above related were not quelled without serious consequences, the discontents continuing from the workmen learning that there was to be found in the statute book an ancient law prohibiting under heavy penalties the use of a machine called a gig mill (though doubts existed as to whether it was the machine which now bore that denomination) and they conceived the project of preventing its further establishment by calling the above statute into operation.

This exactly states the position following the failure of the riots in Wiltshire, and after the tragic death of Helliker[32], the workers there, in combination with the small clothiers in Yorkshire, decided to petition Parliament to put into force these various statutes that had for so long been neglected.

This combination of two rather different groups of people, the workers and the clothiers, was interesting, and did lead the Government to consider the case with more care than it might otherwise have done. The Government would have squashed the workers in the West by immediately abolishing the statute if the latter had acted on their own, but it had considerable sympathy with the small clothiers of the West Riding, regarded as a most hard-working and reliable section of the community; not until it was satisfied that they would not be harmed were the statutes in fact repealed.

The 1806 Report continued:

But your committee would be wanting to the important subject entrusted to their consideration if they were to forebear

49

remarking that if the principles on which the use of these particular machines is objected to were once admitted it would be impossible to draw the line or to foresee the fateful extent of their application. No one will deny that if parliament had acted on such principles fifty years ago the woollen manufacture would never have attained to half its present size. The rapid and prodigious increase of late years in the manufacture and commerce of this country is universally known as well as the effects of that increase by revenue and national strength; and in considering the immediate cause of that augmentation it will appear that under the favour of providence it is principally to be abscribed to the general spirit of enterprise and industry among a free and enlightened people left to the unrestrained exercise of their talents in the employment of a vast capital; pushing to the utmost the principle of the division of labour; calling on all the resources of scientific research and mechanical ingenuity; and finally availing themselves of all the benefits to be derived from visiting foreign countries; not only for forming new and confirming old commercial connections but for obtaining a personal knowledge of the wants, the tastes, the habits, the discoveries, the improvements, the production and the direction of other civilised nations and by thus bringing home facts and suggestions perfecting our existing manufactures, adding new ones to our domestic stock; opening at the same time new markets for the products of our manufacturing and commercial industry and qualifying ourselves for supplying them.

The virtues of free trade, and the importance of utilising new methods and of seeing what one's competitors are doing have rarely been more clearly stated. The Report goes on to argue that these old statutes must therefore be abolished, and it allowed itself to be persuaded that this could be done without any harm to the Yorkshire domestic clothier. That it might harm the woollen worker of the West seemed to occasion little worry.

The evidence given before the 1806 committee enables one to follow the changes that were taking place in the Yorkshire industry. From it, W. C. Crump[33] singled out three clothiers as being typical of the woollen trade: James Ellis of Armley, Joseph Coops of

Pudsey and Ronald Cookson of Holbeck.

Whereas the West of England workers, after their failure in 1806 to get Parliament to enforce the existing statutes, rather abandoned hope, this was not the case in Yorkshire, where the later riots were more serious. Similarly, it is noticeable that whereas in 1802-3 the West of England clothiers tended to lead the way, later the initiative in the parliamentary struggle passed from them to the large Yorkshire merchants. During the next series of riots against machines, those known as the Luddite riots in the years 1810-13, there was no sign of trouble in the West, although Yorkshire was one of the main centres.

Benjamin Gott

It was Benjamin Gott[34] who broke completely through the bounds previously confining the Yorkshire woollen trade; the latter owes much to him, particularly in its factory development.

The recent demolition of Gott's premises at Bean Ing Mills, Wellington Street, Leeds, will have brought this to the mind of all interested in the history of the Yorkshire woollen trade. It was the earliest factory in Leeds; the street frontage of brick was fifty-four bays long, with a three-part archway and a cupola on top. Benjamin Gott began building it in 1794 and completed the first part the following year; it was wood-framed, as was the custom of the time. Ten years later he added a second part with cast-iron columns and consequently less fire risk; finally a third part, completely iron-framed, was built in the 1820s. All who remember this building which until recently was almost unchanged, will realise that it was an unusual and important piece of industrial architecture. Bean Ing Mills illustrated the development of mill architecture between 1790 and 1830; individual mills differ in detail but there is a remarkable general similarity amongst them. They are usually rectangular because spinning machinery fitted better into such a building, and they are noticeably less ornate than contemporary West of England mills.

Comparatively little has been written about these mills, and it is difficult to discover a great deal—most of the early ones were built to the plans of the owners themselves and there appear to have been

51

no industrial architects at the time. Taken as a whole, they are worthy monuments to the men who made the modern Yorkshire woollen and worsted trades.

Benjamin Gott had served his apprenticeship with the firm of Wormald & Fountaine who, with Denisons and Bischoffs, were the largest merchants in the trade. His apprenticeship cost him £400; when this was completed at the age of twenty-two he became a partner. He bought an eleventh part of the firm for £3,660, the older partners retaining the rest; they were allowed to take £60 out of the till each month whereas Gott himself could only take £12. As a merchant he bought from the small domestic clothiers; later he decided to become a manufacturer himself. Like other merchants, he had often supplemented his purchases at the cloth halls by having pieces manufactured by the domestic clothiers to his own instructions. The coming of machinery convinced him that there was a great opportunity for the go-ahead merchant of the eighteenth century to become the great mill owner of the nineteenth. Already he had his own finishing shop, whereas some other merchants employed commission finishers.

These Leeds merchants of the last half of the eighteenth century were good business men. They travelled widely in search of orders, calling regularly on both their customers and the shippers who sent their goods abroad, discussing the many matters concerning finance and future designs just like the manufacturer does today. Occasionally, like the modern manufacturer, they combined these journeys with a holiday.

The history of the woollen trade in Yorkshire in the first part of the nineteenth century, as far as it relates to the type of cloth produced, divides into two distinct sections: the attempt to rival the West of England in making superfine broadcloths, and the development of the cheaper types of fabrics. The future lay mainly with the second section, and increasingly the more expensive cloths sold were worsteds. This trend was not however very apparent during the period when Gott was building his mill, and his importance in the Yorkshire trade, as far as the type of cloth produced is considered, lay in the fact that he was the first to introduce Spanish and Saxony wool in any quantity into manufacturing there. This enabled him to compete with, and in many ways beat, the West of England manufacturers whose traditional business it had been.

By 1800 Gott at Bean Ing was one of the dozen largest employers of labour in the country. As far as the woollen and worsted trades were concerned he stood entirely alone, being the only one to employ over 1,000 workers, of which half were men and 25 per cent each women and children.

Although Gott's success in introducing the manufacture of high-class broadcloth into Yorkshire was perhaps regarded as his most outstanding contribution to the trade, his part in bringing the factory system to the woollen trade is his most permanent memorial, and he is best remembered in history for his connection with the riots that so disturbed the time. The struggle, as has already been stated, started around the shearing frame, and for a time the organised workers were successful in preventing its use. Gott himself was keen to avoid trouble and moved slowly, being aware that the rapid introduction of machinery would lead to trouble. On one occasion he wrote to the Mayor of Leeds that he was prepared to dismantle the machines he had erected so as to prevent such horrid outrages occurring in Yorkshire as had been practised in the West. Later, however, Gott was successful in slowly introducing more types of machinery into his factory; he claimed that the labour involved in producing yarn was reduced by 80 per cent. He had shop looms but none were driven by power, and consequently these costs were not reduced. By 1828 the total labour charge in making a piece of super-fine broadcloth had come down from £9 to £4 7s (£4.35), which shows how expensive the old hand methods of yarn producing had been.

Benjamin Gott often gave evidence at the many parliamentary enquiries made into the state of the woollen trade at the time, and these reveal a man well-informed in all aspects of the trade. He told the House of Lords committee enquiring into the state of the wool trade in 1828 that 'the price of an article when in a complete state of manufacture for sale would be the price of wool plus 50 per cent'. This figure shows that despite the expense of hand-processing, the cost of the wool was the real cause for the high price of fine woollen cloth. Today the position is nearly reversed, and the price would be that of the wool plus 200 per cent.

By the time he died in February 1848, at the age of seventy-eight, there were signs that the long-established broadcloth was falling into disfavour. Partly because of this, and partly because the second generation lacked the great business initiative of the father, the business declined—one of the sons excelled more as a collector of prints, paintings and books than as a cloth manufacturer. Of the third generation, one was Vicar of Leeds and later Bishop of Truro, and with these the Gott family gave up manufacturing.

1830-58

It is appropriate at this point to sum up the position of the Yorkshire woollen and worsted trades in 1830. With the important exception of combing and hand-loom weaving, all processes had gone into the factories. Power-weaving was already applied with some success to the worsted trade, where the stronger yarns made it possible—particularly if cotton warps were being used—but it had not affected the woollen trade.

The slow mechanisation of the Yorkshire woollen and worsted trade continued between 1830 and the year that Baines wrote his survey. As far as the woollen section was concerned, the mule replaced the jenny, but until the coming of the condenser the laborious hand-piecing of the sliver continued. Hand weaving remained an important section of the industry even when Baines was writing his first account, but after 1835-40 the more technically advanced firms had realised that power-loom weaving would come to the woollen industry just as it had to the worsted, and earlier still to the cotton. It was simply a question of developing a power loom with a less harsh movement which would cope with the softer and weaker woollen yarns.

With worsteds the main hold-up to full mechanisation lay in the early combing process. Cartwright, of power-loom fame, had experimented with a combing machine and did in fact invent three. One of these was particularly remembered because of its name, 'Big Ben', after a famous prizefighter—the crank of the machine was said to resemble his arm. But despite a great deal of effort it was not until the middle of the century that a really successful combing machine was made. This was the work of the famous entrepreneur Lister, later Lord Masham, who made full use of the inventive work of such men as Donisthorpe, Holden and the somewhat nebulous Noble, whose name has acquired a permanent place in fame by being attached to the comb in most common use today.

Consequently, by the time that Baines wrote, the Industrial Revolution had virtually completed its long run in the wool-textile trade, but the memory of the craft occupations still lingered and, perhaps more important, still formed the basis of the newly mechanised processes. It was this which gave interest and immediacy to Baines's account of an industry which had been Britain's most important and which although by then taking second place to cotton was still vital to the country's economy.

Notes to Introduction

1 Leach, A. F. (editor), *Beverley Town Documents.*
2 Pirenne, H., *The Economic and Social History of Mediaeval Europe,* 1936, especially p 94 et seq and p 166 et seq.
3 Heaton, H., *The Yorkshire Woollen and Worsted Industry from the Earliest Times up to the Industrial Revolution,* 1920, is the standard work on the subject. The recent second impression contains a new preface giving considerable bibliographical material.
4 Heaton, H., op cit, p 30.
5 Carus-Wilson, E. M., 'The English Cloth Trade in the 12th and 13th Centuries', *Economic History Review,* vol 14, reprinted in *Mediaeval Merchant Venturers.*
6 Bickley, F. (editor), *The Little Red Book of Bristol,* 1900, 2 vols.
7 Kerseys: the name derives from the East Anglian cloth-making town of that name; the West Riding versions were sometimes called Northern Dozens.
8 The classic paper on this subject is Carus Wilson, E. M., 'An Industrial Revolution in the 13th Century', *Economic History Review,* vol 11, reprinted in *Mediaeval Merchant Venturers.* For a more technical approach see Curwen, E. Cecil, 'The Problem of the Early Water Wheel', *Antiquity,* vol 18. The whole period is excellently surveyed in Carus-Wilson, E. M., 'The

Woollen Industry' in Postan, M. and Rich, E. E. (editors), *The Cambridge Economic History of Europe*, vol 2, 1952, pp 355-428.

9 See Wheater, W., 'The Ancient Cloth Trade', *Old Yorkshire*, 2nd Series.

10 Heaton, H., op cit, pp 58-9.

11 Quoted by Miss Sellers in 'Social Economic History', p 45, *Victoria County History, Yorkshire*, from York Municipal Records.

12 For the Aulnage accounts, see Carus-Wilson, E. M., 'The Aulnage Account', *Economic History Review*, vol 2.

13 Heaton, H., op cit, p 69.

14 Heaton, H., op cit, p 85.

15 For the effects of the Tudor legislation on the trade, see Ramsay, G. D., *The Wiltshire Woollen Industry in the 16th and 17th Centuries*, 1943. The analysis made there applies far more widely than to the Wiltshire area.

16 Heaton, H., op cit, p 92.

17 The Halifax Act of 1555, 2 & 3 Philip & Mary, c 13. The preamble is interesting:

> For as much as the parish of Halifax and other places there to adjoining, being planted in the great waste and moors, where the fertility of the ground is not apt to bring forth any corn or good grass but in rare places, and by exceeding and great industry of the inhabitants, and the same inhabitants altogether do live by cloth making, for the great part of them neither getting corn nor able to keep a horse to carry wools, nor yet to buy much wool at once, but have ever used only to repair to the town of Halifax and some others nigh there-unto, and there to buy upon the wool-dryver, some a stone, some two, and some three or four according to their ability, and to carry the same to their houses, some three, four, five and six miles upon their heads and back, and so to make and convert the same either into yarn or cloth and to sell the same, and so to buy more wool of the wool dryver, by means of which industry the barren grounds in those parts be now much inhabited and also 500 households there newly increased within 40 years part.

18 Heaton, H., op cit, p 206.

19 See Friss, A., *Alderman Cockayne's Project and the Cloth Trade*. James I gave Alderman Cockayne a monopoly to dye and finish all cloths in England, and the white or undyed broadcloth trade collapsed, causing great distress in the Westcountry.

The whole economic and social background to the early

Stuarts' intervention in cloth-making, and of course other facets
of the nation's economy, have been brilliantly analysed in two
modern classics: Tawnay's bibliography of Lionel Cranfield
entitled *Business and Politics under James I*, 1950, and more
recently Prestwick, M., *Politics and Profits under the Early
Stuarts, the Career of Lionel Cranfield, Earl of Middlesex.*

20 This and the other interesting trials are summarised in Heaton,
H., op cit, chapter 6, 'Some Milestones in the 17th Century'.

21 Two lines of verse 38—there are 104 verses in all—of a Methodist hymn. See *The Progress of the Gospels in Yorkshire and
other Parts*, 1751, by William Darney.

22 See figures given by Heaton, H., op cit, pp 280-1.

23 The best example is in Thomas Street, Halifax, and was built
by Thomas Bradley in 1775. Pevsner, N., in his *Buildings of
England; Yorkshire—the West Riding*, p 231, rightly comments
'The most noteworthy architectural monument of Halifax'.

24 Daniel Bourn invented the rotary card in 1748, Patent no 628.
Lewis Paul followed later in the same year with another of
quite different conception, Patent no 636.

25 Report of the *Select Committee appointed to Consider the State
of the Woollen Manufacture in England*, Report 1806, vol 3.

26 There is an excellent introduction to the development of spinning in *Wool Research 1918-48*, vol 6, 'Drawing and Spinning'.
Chapter 1 is 'The Development of Drawing and Spinning';
Chapter 2 is 'The Development of Worsted Drawing'. Although
not stated in the volume, these are the work of H. Lemon, who
has now developed his ideas in *Textile History*, vol 1, David &
Charles, autumn 1968.

27 As this may reasonably claim to be the most revolutionary
patent ever produced in the machine development of textiles, it
should be quoted in full:

> The said machine, engine or invention will spin wool or cotton
> into thread, yarn, or worsted which, before it is placed therein
> must be prepared in manner following—all those sorts of wool or
> cotton which it is necessary to card must have each card full,
> batt or roll joined together so as to make the mass become a kind
> of rope or thread of raw wool: In that sort of wool which it is
> necessary to comb, commonly called jersey, a strict regard must
> be had to make the sliver of wool or cotton thus prepared, one
> end of the mass, rope, thread or sliver is put betwixt the pair of

rollers, cylinders or cones, or some such movement, which, being twined round by their own motion, draws in the raw mass of wool or cotton to be spun, in proportion to the velocity given to such rollers, cylinders or cones. As this prepared mass passes regularly through or betwixt these rollers, cylinders or cones, a succession of other rollers, cylinders or cones, moving proportionately faster than the first, draw the rope, thread or sliver into any degree of fineness which may be required. Sometimes the succession of rollers, cylinders or cones (but not the first) have another rotation besides that which diminishes the thread, yarn or worsted (viz:) that they give it a small degree of twist, betwixt each pair, by means of the thread itself passing through the axis or centre of each rotation. In some cases only the first pair of rollers, cylinders or cones are used, and then the bobbin, spool or quill upon which the thread, yarn or worsted is spun, is so contrived as to draw faster than the first roller, cylinder or cones, give, and in such proportion as the first mass, rope or sliver is proposed to be diminished.

28   There is an interesting sidelight on the use made of Paul's inventions. Both that for carding and that for spinning appear in 'The Fleece', the work of a minor poet, James Dyer. They suggest that he had seen the machine working. Of the card already described he wrote:

> But patient art,
> That on experience works from hour to hour,
> Sagacious has a spiral engine formed
> Which on a hundred spools a hundred threads
> With one huge wheel by laps of water turns
> Few hands requiring; easy tended work
> Copiously supplies the greedy looms.

The poet's footnote reads: 'Paul's engine for cotton and for wool'.

Turning to the spinning inventor, he wrote:

> We next are shown,
> A circular machine of new design,
> In conic shape; it draws and spins a thread,
> Without the tedious toil of needless hands,
> A wheel invisible beneath the floor,
> To every member of harmonious frame
> Gives necessary motion. One, intent,
> O'er looks the work; the carded wool, he says
> Is smoothly lapped around these cylinders,
> Which gently turning, yielded to yon cirque
> Of upright spindles, which, with rapid whirl,
> Spin out in long extent an even twine.

The poet in this case notes: 'A circular machine, a most curious piece of apparatus'.

29 'The Transference of the Worsted Industry from Norfolk to the West Riding', *Economic Journal*, 1910.
30 See Atkinson (editor), *Some Aspects of the 18th Century Woollen and Worsted Trade in Halifax*.
31 Budding's history has recently been elucidated in Randall, H. A., 'Some Mid Gloucestershire Engineers and Inventors', *Newcomen Society Transactions*, vol 27, 1965-6.
32 Helliker was a young clothier who probably led an attack on Littleton Mill. He was arrested at an identity parade in Trowbridge and sentenced to death at Salisbury Assizes.
33 Crump, W. C., *History of the Leeds Woollen Industry*.
34 See Heaton, H., 'Benjamin Gott and The Industrial Revolution', *Economic History Review*, vol 3.

Bibliography

Notes on books in alphabetical list below

As befits the country's oldest industry, the bibliography of the Yorkshire woollen and worsted industry is considerable. In addition to Baines, three nineteenth-century works remain important: Bischoff, J., *Comprehensive History of Woollen and Worsted Manufacture*, 2 vols, 1842; Burnley, J., *History of Wool and Worsted Combing*, 1889; and James, J., *History of Worsted Manufacture*, 1857. In addition there are several topographical books containing valuable accounts of textile processes and traditions, in particular Lawson, J., *Progress in Pudsey* and Hodgson, *Textile Manufacture in Keighley*.

It was not until 1920, however, that a really satisfactory history of the trade was produced and Heaton's *The Yorkshire Woollen and Worsted Industry from the Earliest Times to the Industrial Revolution* has remained the chief authority. A recent reprint contains a valuable new bibliographical note by the author. It is one of the tragedies of the history of the trade that Professor Heaton's departure many years ago to America has meant that he has neither been able to revise his outstanding volume or, even more unfortunate, to write the sequel. His essay on Benjamin Gott, in volume 3 of *Economic History Review* shows what we have missed. Otherwise, the best work between the wars was probably that done under the influence of W. C. Crump. He himself edited and largely wrote *The Leeds Woollen Industry, 1760-1820*, and with Mrs G. Ghorbal the even better *History of the Huddersfield Woollen Industry*. Fortunately J. L. & B. Hammond devoted a large section of their well known *The Skilled Labourer* to the Yorkshire trade and this remains the best account we have of the Industrial Revolution in the area.

During the late 1930s and 1940s Professor E. M. Carus-Wilson, in essays published originally in the *Economic History Review* and then reprinted in her *Mediaeval Merchant Venturers*, reinterpreted the position of the English cloth trade as a whole. This necessarily changed our opinion of the Yorkshire industry, although one must realise that the real growth of the Yorkshire trade came several centuries after Professor Carus-Wilson's main interest.

Since 1950 many volumes have been written in which the Yorkshire woollen industry plays a part, but the number of books solely devoted to it remains surprisingly few. E. Sigsworth's *Black Dyke Mills* is probably the outstanding volume, mainly because the first three chapters provide by far the best survey there is of the worsted trade in the nineteenth century.

Many contributions to scholarly journals are listed in the bibliography. But they have tended to be written more about economic developments in general than the Yorkshire trade in particular. Large areas remain unexplored. Except for Sigsworth's volume already mentioned (Black Dyke Mill is John Foster's of Queensbury) none of the other famous firms in the trade have been adequately described. Salts of Saltaire and Lister's of Manningham are two such examples.

Probably in the final resort the industry has been best brought to life in Miss Phyllis Bentley's well known and delightful novels; and in this field T. Armstrong's *The Crowthers of Bankdam* must be mentioned.

Armstrong, T.	*The Crowthers of Bankdam.* 1940
Ashley, W. J.	*The Early History of the English Woollen Trade.* 1887
Ashton, T. S.	*The Industrial Revolution 1760-1830.* 1948
Aspinall, A. E.	*The Early English Trade Unions.* 1949
Atkinson, F. (editor)	*Some Aspects of the 18th Century Woollen and Worsted Trade of Halifax.* 1956
Bateson, M.	'Review of Beverley Town Documents', *English Historical Review* 1894
Beckwith, F.	'The Population of Leeds during the Industrial Revolution', *Thoresby Society*, miscellaneous vol 112

Bentley, P.   *Inheritance*

Bischoff, J.   *Comprehensive History of Woollen and Worsted Manufacture*, 2 vols. 1842

Bland, H. E.   *English Economic History. Selected docu-*
Brown, P. A. &   *ments.* 1933
Tawnay, R. H. (editors)

Bowden, P. J.   *The Wool Trade in Tudor and Stuart England.* 1959

Bowden, P. J.   'Wool Supply and the Woollen Industry', *Economic History Review*, vol LX no 1, 1956

Burnley, J.   *History of Wool and Wool Combing.* 1889

Carus-Wilson, E. M. *Mediaeval Merchant Venturers.* 1954

Carus-Wilson, E. M. 'The Woollen Industry', *The Cambridge Economic History of Europe*, vol 2, edited by Postan, M. & Rich, E. E. 1952

Carus-Wilson, E. M. 'An Industrial Revolution in the 13th Century', *Economic History Review*, vol 2, reprinted in *Mediaeval Merchant Venturers*

Carus-Wilson, E. M. 'Evidence of Industrial Growth on Some 15th Century Manors, *Economic History Review*, 2nd series, vol 12. 1959

Carus-Wilson, E. M. 'The Aulnage Accounts', *Economic History Review*, vol 2

Carus-Wilson, E. M. 'The English Cloth Trade in the 12th and 13th Centuries, *Economic History Review*, vol 14

Carus-Wilson, E. M. 'Trends in the Export of English Woollens in the 14th Century', *Economic History Review*, new series, vol 3

Carus-Wilson, E. M. *England's Export Trade 1274-1547.* 1963
& Coleman, O.

Clapham, J. H.   *Woollen and Worsted Industries.* 1907

Clapham, J. H.   *An Economic History of Modern Britain*, 3 vols

Clapham, J. H.   'Industrial Organisation of the Yorkshire Woollen and Worsted Industries', *Economic Journal*, vol 16. 1906

Clapham, J. H.	'The Transference of the Worsted Industry from the East Anglia to the West Riding', *Economic Journal*. 1910
Crump, W. C.	*The Leeds Woollen Industry 1760-1820*. 1931
Crump, W. C. & Ghorbal, G.	*History of the Huddersfield Woollen Industry*. 1935
Davis, R.	'English Foreign Trade 1660-1700', *Economic History Review*, 2nd series, vol 7. 1954
Davis, R.	'English Foreign Trade 1700-1774', *Economic History Review*, 2nd series, vol 15. 1962
Defoe, D.	*Tour Through Great Britain*
Fiennes, C.	*Journeys* (c 1685-1703), ed Morris, C. 1947
Fisher, F. J.	'Commercial Trends and Policies in 17th Century England', *Economic History Review*, vol 10. 1940
Fisher, F. J.	'London's Export Trade in the Early 17th Century', *Economic History Review*, 2nd series, vol 3. 1950
Friis, A.	*Alderman Cockayne's Project and the Cloth Trade*. 1927
Gray, H. L.	'The Production & Exportation of English Woollens in the 14th Century', *English Historical Review*. Jan 1924
Hammond, J. L. & B.	*The Town Labourer*. 1920
Hammond, J. L. & B.	*The Skilled Labourer*. 1920
Heaton, H.	'The Assessment of Wages in the West Riding of Yorkshire in the 17th and 18th Centuries', *Economic Journal*. 1914
Heaton, H.	*The Yorkshire Woollen and Worsted Industry from the Earliest Times to the Industrial Revolution*. 1920
Heaton, H.	'The Leeds White Cloth Hall', *Thoresby Society*, vol XXII
Heaton, H.	'Benjamin Gott and the Industrial Revolution in Yorkshire', *Economic History Review*, vol 3

Heaton, H.	'Tricks of the Trade', *Thoresby Society*, vol XXII
Heaton, H. (editor)	*The Letter Book of Joseph Holroyd & Sam Hill*
Hinton, R. W. K.	*The Eastern Trade and the Commonwealth*. 1959
Hodgson, —.	*Textile Manufacture in Keighley*. 1878
James, J.	*History of Worsted Manufacture*. 1857
James, J.	*History and Topography of Bradford*. 1841
Jubb, S.	*History of the Shoddy Trade*
Lawson, J.	*Progress in Pudsey*
Leach, A. F. (editor)	*Beverley Town Documents*. 1900
Lemon, H.	'Some Aspects of the Early History of Spinning with Special Reference to Wool', *Journal of the Textile Institute*. Aug 1952
Ling Roth, A. H.	'Hand Card Making', *Bankfield Museum Notes*, 1st series, no XI
Ling Roth, A. H.	'Hand Combing', *Bankfield Museum Notes*, 1st series, no VI
Ling Roth, A. H.	'Bishop Blaise, Saint, Martyr and Wool Combers' Patron, *Bankfield Museum Notes*, 2nd series, no VI
Lipson, E.	*An Economic History of England*, 3 vols. 1943-5
Lister, J.	'Notes on the Early History of the Woollen Trade in Bradford and Halifax', *Bradford Antiquary*, vol 2
Parliamentary Report	*Report of the Select Committee on the Petition of Merchants and Manufacturers in the Woollen Manufacture of Yorkshire*. Reports 1802-3, vol 5
Parliamentary Report	*Report of the Select Committee appointed to Consider the State of the Woollen Manufacture in England*. Report 1806, vol 3
Parliamentary Report	*Report of the House of Lords Enquiry concerning the Wool Trade*. 1828
Parliamentary Report	*Reports on the Condition of the Hand Loom Weavers*. Reports 1835, vol XII; Reports

	1839, vol XIII; Reports 1840, vol XXII; Reports 1840, vol XXIV
Pevsner, N.	*The Buildings of England. Yorkshire—The West Riding.* 1959
Pirenne, H.	*The Economic and Social History of Mediaeval Europe.* 1936
Ramsay, G. D.	*English Foreign Trade during the 17th Century*
Ramsay, G. D.	*The Wiltshire Woollen Industry in the 16th and 17th Centuries.* 1943
Sellers, M.	'Economic History of Yorkshire', *Victoria County History, Yorkshire,* vol 3
Sellers, M.	'The Textile Industries', *Victoria County History, Yorkshire,* vol 2
Sellers, M.	*Yorkshire Merchants and Merchant Adventurers (1356-1917).* 1918
Sigsworth, E.	*Black Dyke Mills.* 1958
Stone, L.	'Elizabethan Overseas Trade', *Economic History Review,* 2nd series, vol 2. 1950
Supple, B. E.	*Commercial Crisis and Change in England 1600-1642.* 1959
Unwin, G.	*Industrial Organisation in the 16th and 17th Centuries.* 1904
Unwin, G.	*Studies in Economic History.* 1927
Wadsworth, A. P. & Mann, J. de L.	*The Cotton Trade in Industrial Lancashire 1600-1780.* 1931
Webb, S. & B.	*History of Trade Unions,* 1902
Wilson, G.	'Cloth Production and International Competition in the 17th Century', *Economic History Review,* 2nd series, vol 12. 1961
WIRA	*Wool Research 1918-48,* vol 4, 'Carding'. Chapter 1 is 'The Development of the Carding Engine'
WIRA	*Wool Research 1918-48,* vol 6, 'Drawing and Spinning'. Chapter 1 is 'The Development of Drawing and Spinning'; Chapter 2 is 'The Development of Worsted Drawing'

E

THE

WOOLLEN MANUFACTURE OF ENGLAND:

WITH SPECIAL REFERENCE TO THE

LEEDS CLOTHING DISTRICT.

By EDWARD BAINES, Esq., M.P.

FROM A PAPER READ BEFORE THE BRITISH ASSOCIATION FOR THE ADVANCEMENT
OF SCIENCE, AT LEEDS, IN 1858.

CHAPTER I.

I.—*Woollen and Worsted Fabrics.*

It will conduce to the understanding of important points in the economy of the manufacture, to explain in the first place the difference between the woollen and the worsted fabrics. The raw material of both is sheep's wool. It would formerly have been sufficient to say that woollens were made of short wool, and worsted goods of long wool; but owing to the improvement in the worsted spinning machinery, much short wool, both English and colonial, is now used in that manufacture. Wool intended for woollens is prepared for spinning by the carding machine; whilst wool intended for worsted goods, being generally of a longer staple, is prepared for spinning by the metallic comb. But the essential distinction of woollens from worsted, cotton, linen, and every other textile fabric is, that they depend upon that peculiar property of sheep's wool, its disposition to *felt*; that is, under pressure and warm moisture, to *interlock its fibres* as by strong mutual attraction, and thus to *run up* into a compact substance not easily separable. Wools differ in the degree of this felting property; but, generally speaking, the long wools possess it in a lower degree than the short wools, and the wools which felt best are the best adapted for making woollen cloth. For worsted stuffs the felting property is not required; and not only have the wools used for this purpose less of the felting property, but they are so treated in the spinning and manufacture as almost entirely to destroy it.

In every other textile fabric, when the material is spun into yarn and woven into a web, the fabric is complete. But in woollen cloth, after the process of spinning and weaving comes the essential process of felting, by means of heavy pressure with soap and warm water; and so efficacious is this process, that a piece of cloth under it often shrinks up to two-thirds its original length and little more than half its width. The process is called milling or fulling, and some of the oldest traces of the woollen manufacture found in ancient records are in the mention of fulling mills on certain streams or estates. Before the milling, the web of the woollen cloth, when held up to the day, admits the light through its crossed threads; but after the milling, every fibre in the piece having laid hold of the neighbouring fibres, and all having firmly interlaced themselves together, the cloth becomes thick and opaque; of course it is made stouter, warmer, and more enduring in the wear; and if torn, it will be found that its tenacity has consisted not so much in the strength of the warp and weft as in the firm adhesion of all the fibres, so that it does not unravel like cotton or linen cloth.

After the cloth has been milled it undergoes the various processes of dressing or finishing, which consist mainly in these two—first, raising up all the fibres of the wool which can be detached by violent and long-continued brushing of the cloth with teazles, so as to make a nap on the surface; and then, secondly, shearing off that nap in a cutting machine, so clean and smooth as to give a soft and almost velvety appearance and feel to the cloth. This nap, more or less closely cut, distinguishes woollen cloth from nearly all other fabrics; it is one of its two essential characters; and, combined with the felting, it makes superfine broad cloth one of the finest, warmest, richest, most useful, and most enduring of all tissues.

But in order to produce these two principal characteristics of woollen cloth, the *felting* and the *nap*, it will easily be seen that woollen yarn must not be spun so tight and hard as worsted, cotton, or linen yarn. The fibres must be left as loose as possible, first, that they may felt, and afterwards that they may constitute a nap. Hence woollen yarn, both for the warp and weft, is spun into a much feebler, looser, and less twisted thread, than other kinds of yarn. But this feebleness of the yarn constitutes a principal difficulty in applying the power-loom to the woollen manufacture. The threads are more liable to break by the passing of the shuttle through them, and the weaving is consequently more difficult. This difficulty is increased by the great width of the web, which in broad cloth, before it is milled, is nine feet. Owing to these combined causes, the power-loom in the woollen manufacture works much more slowly than in the worsted manufacture; in the latter, on the average, the shuttle flies at the rate of 160 picks per minute, whilst the power-loom in weaving broad cloth only makes 40 to 48 picks per minute—that is, just the same as the hand-loom. The weaving of woollen cloth by hand is a man's work, whereas the weaving of cotton, linen, or silk cloth by hand was a woman's or a child's work. Hence the hand-loom weaver in the woollen manufacture has never been reduced to the miserable wages paid to the same class of operatives in other manufactures, and hence he maintains a more equal competition with the steam-loom. It is to this cause that we must principally ascribe *the continued existence of the system of domestic manufacture in the woollen trade;* and to the same cause we must ascribe the slower advances made in the woollen than in those manufactures *where all the processes can be more advantageously carried on in factories, by one vast system of machinery, under a single eye, and by the power of great capital.* Whether for good or for evil, or for a combination of both, such are the economical results which may be traced in a great measure to the peculiarities in woollen yarn and cloth.

II.—*Woollen Manufacture—Processes.*

But another circumstance must be noticed, as bearing upon the same results, namely, that the processes of the woollen manufacture are more numerous and complex than those of any other of our textile manufactures. In one of those complete and beautiful establishments where fine cloth is both manufactured and finished, as that of Messrs. Benjamin Gott and Sons, of Leeds, which has long ranked with the first woollen factories of any country, the spectator who may be admitted to it will see all the following processes, namely:—

1. Sorting the wool—no less than ten different qualities being found in a single fleece.
2. Scouring it with a lye and hot water, to remove the grease and dirt.
3. Washing it with clean cold water.
4. Drying it, first in an extractor—a rapidly revolving machine full of holes, and next, by spreading it and exposing it to the heat of steam.

71

5. Dyeing, when the cloth is to be wool-dyed.
6. Willying, by revolving cylinders armed with teeth, to open the matted locks and free them from dust.
7. Teasing, with a teaser or devil, still further to open and clean.
8. Sprinkling plentifully with olive oil, to facilitate the working of the wool.
9. Moting, with the moting-machine, to take off the motes or burs, *i.e.*, seeds of plants or grasses which adhere to the fleece.
10. Scribbling, in a scribbling machine, consisting of a series of cylinders clothed with cards or wire brushes working upon each other, the effect of which is still further to disentangle the wool and draw out the fibres.
11. Plucking, in a plucking machine, more effectually to mix up the different qualities which may remain in the wool.
12. Carding, in a carding machine, resembling the scribbler, but more perfectly opening the wool, spreading it of a regular thickness and weight, reducing it to a light, filmy substance, and then bringing it out in cardings or slivers about three feet in length.
13. Slubbing, at a frame called the billey, generally containing sixty spindles, where the cardings are joined to make a continuous yarn, drawn out, slightly twisted, and wound on bobbins.
    By a new machine, called the Condenser, attached to the carding machine, the wool is brought off in a continuous sliver, wound on cylinders, and ready to be conveyed to the mule, so as to dispense with the billey.
14. Spinning on the mule, which contains from 300 to 1000 spindles per pair.
15. Reeling the yarn intended for the warp.
16. Warping it, and putting it on the beam for the loom.
17. Sizing the warp with animal gelatine, to facilitate the weaving.
18. Weaving at the power-loom or hand-loom.
19. Scouring the cloth with fuller's earth, to remove the oil and size.
20. Dyeing, when piece-dyed.

21. Burling, to pick out irregular threads, hairs, or dirt.
22. Milling or fulling, with soap and warm water, either in the fulling-stocks or in the improved milling machine, where it is squeezed between rollers.
23. Scouring, to remove the soap.
24. Drying and stretching on tenters.
25. Raising the nap of the cloth, by brushing it strongly on the gig with teazles fixed upon cylinders.
26. Cutting or shearing off the nap in two cutting-machines, one cutting lengthwise of the piece and the other across.
27. Boiling the cloth, to give it a permanent face.
28. Brushing, in a brushing machine.
29. Pressing in hydraulic presses, sometimes with heat.
30. Cutting the nap a second time.
31. Burling and drawing, to remove defects, and marking with the manufacturer's name.
32. Pressing a second time.
33. Steaming, to take away the liability to spot.
34. Folding or cutting for the warehouse.

These processes, as has been said, are greatly more numerous than those required by any other textile manufacture, and they are performed by a much greater variety of machines and of work-people. It is pretty obvious that there must be proportionate difficulty in effecting improvements which will tell materially on the quantity or the price of the goods produced.

III.—Dearness of the Raw Material.

There is still another fact which retards the advance of the woollen, as compared with other manufactures, namely, the higher price of the raw material. The average value of the sheep's wool imported during the three years 1854, 1855, and 1856, was 1s. 4d. per lb., and the average price of English wool in the same year was about 1s. 2d. per lb.; but during those three years the average price of cotton wool imported was only 5¾d. per lb., and that of flax only 5d. per lb.* So that wool is about three times the market price of the two vegetable substances which form the raw materials of the cotton and linen manufactures. Nor can sheep's wool be augmented in quantity so rapidly as raw materials which merely require the cultivation of the soil. The fleece, at least in this country, forms only a small proportion of the value of the sheep on which it grows; and the sheep farmer is more dependent on the demand for his mutton than on the demand for his wool. Now the consumption of animal food only increases, as a general rule, with the increase of population; and hence there is a natural restriction on the supply of sheep's wool, owing to which restriction the price is kept high.

IV.—*Factories, Woollen and Worsted.*

But the economist may inquire—how is it that the worsted manufacture has of late years increased so much more rapidly than the woollen, seeing that it uses the same raw material, sheep's wool? I may briefly say, that it is to be ascribed in part to very remarkable improvements made within these few years in the process of Combing, which is now performed by machinery, instead of by hand, reducing the cost of the process almost to nothing; in part to the greater simplicity of the other processes, admitting of their being carried on almost entirely in large factories; but more than all to the introduction of cotton warps into the manufacture, which has not only cheapened the raw material, but has introduced a vast variety of new descriptions of goods, light, beautiful, cheap, and adapted both for dress and furniture.

I am informed by a Bradford merchant of great knowledge, that "out of 100 pieces of worsted goods manufactured, at least 95 are made with cotton warps; and a rough estimate of the cotton contained would be, that if a piece weighed 3 lbs., one pound weight

* It will be seen from the Annual Statement of the Trade and Navigation of the United Kingdom for 1856, that for the three years 1854, 1855, and 1856, the average import of sheep's wool was 107,211,277 lbs., of the computed real value of 7,230,249*l.* (showing 1s. 4d. per lb.); of cotton, 934,323,824 lbs., of the value of 22,490,711*l.* (showing 5¾d. per lb.); and of flax, 164,405,248 lbs., of the value of 3,461,899*l.* (showing 5d. per lb.), pp. 11 to 16. I am assured by practical men that the scales of prices by which the values are computed are very correct.

would be cotton and the rest wool." There is still, therefore, a greater weight of wool than of cotton in those goods; but as cotton warps are stronger than woollen, owing to their being harder spun, even when their weight is less, the cloth may be made altogether much lighter than worsted goods were formerly made, and thus the material is economized.

If we look to the factory return made by the factory inspectors in 1856, and printed by the House of Commons in 1857, we shall find that in Yorkshire there were 445 worsted factories and 806 woollen factories; but the number of operatives was 78,994 in the former, and only 42,982 in the latter. The average number of operatives in the worsted factories therefore was 177, whilst in the woollen factories it was only 53. The whole number of operatives returned in the census of 1851, as employed in these two manufactures in the county of York, was 97,147 in the worsted manufacture, and 81,128 in the woollen. Four-fifths of all the hands employed in the worsted trade are in factories, whilst only about half of those in the woollen trade are in factories.

Everything tends to show that the worsted manufacture, like those of cotton and linen, has become an employment carried on by the machinery of large factories; and as mechanical improvements are constantly speeding the power-loom and the spindle,—so that in worsted factories the power-loom has increased 67 per cent.* in speed within the last ten years, and the spindle 114 per cent.—manufactures thus situated must advance more rapidly than those which, like the woollen, are more dependent on manual labour.

V.—Persons, &c., Employed, 1838 and 1856.

The woollen manufacture, though large, prosperous, and advancing with considerable rapidity, has within the last twenty years advanced less rapidly than any of the other great textile manufactures. It was surpassed by the cotton manufacture at the beginning of the century. It still holds the second place in regard to the

* Ten years ago the average speed of worsted looms was 96 picks per minute; it is now 160. In the old spinning frame, called the fly frame, generally used ten years since, the spindles made 2800 revolutions per minute: in the new frame, called the bell frame, they make 6000.

number of operatives employed, though not to the number employed in factories, in which it is surpassed both by the worsted and the flax or linen trades.

The following table shows the advances made by all the textile manufactures, in respect to number of operatives, horse-power, and power-looms, from 1838 to 1856. It will be seen that in the woollen mills, between 1838 and 1856, the number of operatives increased 44 per cent., the horse-power employed increased 25 per cent., and the number of power-looms increased 572 per cent.; but still the other manufactures advanced with greater strides in almost all these respects.

(A.)—FACTORIES OF THE UNITED KINGDOM IN 1838 AND 1856.

Description of Factories.	Persons Employed.			Horse-power.			Power-looms.		
	1838.	1856.	Incr.	1838.	1856.	Incr.	1836.*	1856.	Incr
	No.	No.	Pr.cnt.	No.	No.	Pr.cnt.	No.	No.	Pr.cnt
Cotton,	259,104	379,213	46	59,803	97,132	62	108,751	298,847	17
Woollen,	54,808	79,091	44	20,617	25,901	25	2,150	14,453	57
Worsted,	31,628	87,794	177	7,176	14,904	108	2,969	38,956	1,21
Flax, .	43,557	80,262	84	11,089	18,322	65	1,714	9,260	44
Silk, .	34,303	56,137	64	3,384	5,176	53	209	7,689	3,57
Totals,	423,400	682,497	61	102,069	161,435	58	115,793	369,205	21

VI.—*Raw Material—Sources of Supply.*

I must now refer to the sources from which the raw material, sheep's wool, is drawn, and to the remarkable changes which the present century has witnessed in regard to it. The wool is English, foreign, and colonial, and comes from all the quarters of the globe. Our largest supply is from the United Kingdom, but nearly half of the domestic wool is consumed in the worsted manufacture, and the other half is used for the lower kinds of woollen goods. Within living memory Yorkshire cloth was made exclusively of English wool, though Spanish wool has long been used for the finer cloths

* The first return of power looms was in 1836. There was also a general factory return in that year; but it bears evident marks of inaccuracy, as pointed out by the factory inspectors in their report of October, 1856.

of the West of England.† Now, however, English wool, from its comparative coarseness, is entirely disused in the making of broad cloth. When the late Mr. Gott (who with the late Mr. James Bischoff and others fought a hard battle for many years, first to get rid of the monstrous duty of 6*d.* per pound on foreign wool imposed in 1819, and afterwards to prevent its re-imposition), told a committee of the House of Lords that broad cloth made of English wool would not be merchantable, and that their lordships' servants would not wear it, the statement was received with a burst of incredulity and derision. But so it was. The cloth of the present day is immensely superior both in fabric and in finish to the cloth of half a century back. Working men now wear finer cloth than gentlemen wore when Mr. Gott began his spirited improvements; and it is so in consequence of the general use of the fine and delicate wool of the Merino sheep. In the last half of the eighteenth century the import of foreign wool fluctuated from a little under to a little over two million pounds weight a year. In 1799 it was 2,263,666 lbs.; but in the year 1857 the quantity of foreign and colonial wool imported was 127,390,885 lbs., of which 90,903,666 lbs. was retained for home consumption. As the exports of woollen goods did not increase in any proportion whatever to these figures, it is evident that the character of the cloth, both that worn at home and that exported, must have changed by the substitution of foreign and colonial for English wool.

The foreign wool first used when the improvement in the quality of the cloth began, was that of Spain, the native country of the Merino sheep. The import of wool sprung up suddenly from 2,263,666 lbs. in 1779 (*sic*), to 8,609,368 lbs. in 1800; and of the latter quantity 6,062,824 lbs., or more than two-thirds, was Spanish. After the French invasion of Spain and the long Peninsular wars, the quality of Spanish wool degenerated, and the quantity fell off; and its place in our manufacture was gradually filled by the wool of Saxony and Silesia, into which countries the Merino breed of sheep had been introduced in the year 1765. The German wool is still by much the finest used in any country; but as the Merino flocks were introduced by Mr. Macarthur into our great Australian

† It is certain, from the facts stated in Smith's Memoirs of Wool (vol. i. p. 196), that Spanish wool was used in England before the year 1656.

colonies, and were found to increase there immensely without any very great degeneracy in the quality of the fleece, German wool has, in its turn, to a very considerable extent been superseded by Australian.

The following table shows the imports and exports of foreign and colonial wool, at intervals of about ten years, for the last century : —

(B.)—FOREIGN AND COLONIAL WOOL IMPORTED INTO AND EXPORTED FROM THE UNITED KINGDOM, FROM 1766 TO 1857—SELECTED YEARS.

Years.	Foreign Wool Imported.	Colonial Wool Imported.	Total Imported.	Foreign and Colonial Wool Exp'd.	Left for Home Cons'ption.
	Lbs.	Lbs.	Lbs.	Lbs.	Lbs.
1766	1,926,000	—	1,926,000	—	1,926,000
1771	1,829,000	—	1,829,000	—	1,829,000
1780	323,000	—	323,000	—	323,000
1790	2,582,000	—	2,582,000	—	2,582,000
1799	2,263,000	—	2,263,000	—	2,263,000
1800	8,609,000	—	8,609,000	—	8,609,000
1810	10,879,000	34,000	10,914,000	—	10,914,000
1820	9,653,000	122,000	9,775,000	64,000	9,711,000
1830	30,303,000	2,002,000	32,305,000	659,000	31,646,000
1840	36,585,000	12,850,000	49,436,000	1,014,000	48,421,000
1850	26,102,000	48,224,000	74,326,000	14,388,000	59,938,000
1855	24,681,000	74,619,000	99,300,000	29,453,000	69,846,000
1857	44,522,000	82,868,000	127,390,000	36,487,000*	90,903,000

Table (C.) shows: The decline in the quantity of Spanish wool imported from 6,062,824 lbs. in 1800, to 383,129 lbs. in 1857 ; the increase of German wool from 412,394 lbs. in 1800, to 26,073,882 lbs. in 1830, and its subsequent decline to 5,993,380 lbs. in 1857 ; the increase of Australian wool from 167 lbs. in 1810, to 49,209,655 lbs. in 1857 ; the increase in South African or Cape wool from 9623 lbs. in 1816, to 14,287,828 lbs. in 1857 ; and the increase in East Indian wool from 67,763 lbs. in 1834, to 19,370,741 lbs. in 1857.

These are remarkable commercial changes, and they warrant the hope that we may ere long find in the East Indies, Australia, and Africa, sources of supply for the still more important raw material

* Of this quantity 31,456,900 lbs. was of colonial wool.

THE WOOLLEN MANUFACTURE OF ENGLAND.

of cotton, produced by the labour of free men, instead of being so dangerously and perniciously dependent on the slave-raised cotton of the United States.†

The changes which have taken place in the sources of supply are shown in the following table:—

(C.)—IMPORTS OF WOOL INTO THE UNITED KINGDOM FROM THE PRINCIPAL COUNTRIES, FOREIGN AND COLONIAL, FROM 1800 TO 1857 —SELECTED YEARS.*

Years.	Spain.	Germany.	Australia.	S. Africa	East Indies
	Lbs.	Lbs.	Lbs.	Lbs.	Lbs.
1800	6,062,000	412,000	—	—	—
1810	5,952,000	778,000	167	—	—
1816	2,958,000	2,816,000	13,611	9,623	—
1820	3,536,000	5,113,000	99,415	29,717	—
1830	1,643,000	26,073,000	1,967,000	33,000	—
1834	2,343,000	22,634,000	3,558,000	141,000	67,000
1840	1,266,000	21,812,000	9,721,000	751,000	2,441,000
1850	440,000	9,166,000	39,018,000	5,709,000	3,473,000
1857	383,000	5,993,000	49,209,000	14,287,000	19,370,000

Of the imports of German wool I must remark that they have fallen off even to a greater extent than appears from the above table, inasmuch as there is now a large quantity of rag wool, called shoddy and mungo, imported from Germany; and I am assured by Mr. Fonblanque, of the Statistical Department of the Board of Trade, that no distinction is made at the custom house between the entries of the finest Saxon wool, which is of the value of 3s. per lb., and those of shoddy, which is only worth a few pence per lb. This is a distinction which ought to be forthwith introduced in the accounts, especially as shoddy, though inferior in value, has become a very important raw material in the woollen manufacture.§

† The above was written in 1858, before the happy abolition of slavery in the United States.
* Periods of ten years are taken, except in the years 1816 and 1834, which are introduced as being the years in which wool was first imported from South Africa and the East Indies.
§ Shoddy is now entered separately from wool.

79

VII.—*British Wool—Annual Produce.*

Of the annual produce of wool in the United Kingdom there are, as has been said, no reliable statistics whatever ; and the judgment of those engaged in the trade varies very widely. The late Mr. John Luccock, a wool merchant of Leeds, and a careful inquirer, in a work published by him in 1800 " On the Nature and Properties of Wool," estimated the number of sheep in England and Wales at 26,147,763, and the quantity of wool produced annually at 94,376,640 lbs. weight. The late Mr. James Hubbard revised this estimate in 1828 for a committee of the House of Lords, with the aid of Sir George Goodman—both of those gentlemen being wool merchants in Leeds—and raised the quantity of wool to 111,160,560 lbs. Professor Low, in his able work " On the Domesticated Animals of the British Islands," published in 1845, estimates the number of sheep in the British Islands at 35,000,000, and the produce of wool at 157,500,000 lbs. Mr. Southey, an eminent wool-broker in London, who has published several works on colonial wool, issued a little work in 1851,† in which, judging from the information he received from wool merchants in Leeds, Bradford, and other places, he raised the estimate to 228,950,000 lbs. ; and then, by an unreliable mode of calculating, even carried it to the enormous figure of 275,000,000 lbs. weight.

The balance of authority would dispose us to conclude that the annual produce of domestic wool must be between 150,000,000 lbs. and 200,000,000 lbs. If we take the medium, viz., 175,000,000 lbs., at 1*s*. 3*d*. per pound., which is about the average price of the last thirty years, the value of this great raw material produced at home will be £10,937,500. The judgment thus formed from comparison of authorities has been exactly and unexpectedly confirmed by the result of careful inquiries and calculations, founded on the number of hands employed, the power of the machinery, and the estimated value of the goods manufactured. That result is, that 160,000,000 lbs. is used by the woollen and worsted manufactures, whilst the quantity exported in 1857 was 15,142,881 lbs., making an aggregate

† Rise, Progress, and Present State of Colonial Sheep and Wools, by Thomas Southey.

of 175, 142,881 lbs. of English wool.

The exports of English wool, both in the raw state and in the first state of manufacture, namely, yarn, are greatly and rapidly increasing, as will be seen by the following table:—

(D.)—BRITISH WOOL AND WOOLLEN AND WORSTED YARN EXPORTED.

Years.	Wool.	Woollen and Worsted Yarn.
	Lbs.	Lbs.
1824	53,000	12,640
1830	2,951,000	1,108,000
1840	4,810,000	3,796,000
1850	12,001,000	13,794,000
1857	15,142,000	24,654,000

Thus the farmer is deriving benefit from the freedom of trade, and English wool is resuming its flow through channels which legislation had closed for five centuries. It is for our manufacturers to take care that no other country makes a better use of their raw material than themselves.

VIII.—*Progress of the Woollen Trade.*

Of the history of this ancient manufacture, up to our own times, I must dispose in a few sentences.

It is probable that the fleece of the sheep afforded the first material of human clothing, and that in this pastoral country it has been manufactured from the earliest dawn of civilization. It is on record that the Romans had weaving establishments of woollen cloth at Winchester; that the mother of Alfred the Great was skilled in the spinning of wool; that Flemish woollen weavers settled in England in the time of William the Conqueror; that fresh immigrations of weavers from Flanders took place in the reigns of Henry I., Henry III., Edward I., and Edward III.; that the last-named king especially encouraged the settlement of these artizans in various parts of the country, and that in this policy he was followed by Henry VII.; and that at the Reformation many thousands of woollen weavers, flying from the persecution of the duke of Alva in the Low Countries, found refuge in England. It is certain that the manufac-

81

F

ture of woollen and worsted goods in Flanders, and of woollens in Italy, was carried to a high degree of perfection long before the art had made any considerable advancement in England. There are also many accounts of the exportation of English wool to those countries from very early times; and it would appear to have been of better quality than that of any other country, except Spain. But the monarchs who endeavoured to establish the woollen manufacture in England, instead of relying on our natural advantages for that branch of industry, sought to attain the end by prohibiting the exportation of the raw material. In the years 1337 and 1341, under Edward III., the export was forbidden by statute, under penalty of life and limb: and from that time forward, for nearly five centuries, the statute book was loaded with Acts, equally absurd and many of them equally severe, to prevent the "running" or illegal exportation of wool. Hundreds, if not thousands, of volumes and pamphlets were issued to show that this was one of the first points of national policy; and that the country would be ruined if we allowed other countries to obtain our wool, instead of manufacturing it ourselves. There are few things in the history of nations showing so entire an ignorance of political economy, and such outrageous blindness in statistics, as the history of the English woollen manufacture. It was not till the year 1824 that English wool was allowed to be exported; and it is amusing to recall the long struggle by which freedom was obtained for the export of our own wool, the import of foreign wool, and the import of foreign cloth—Lord Liverpool, Mr. Robinson, and Mr. Huskisson having alternately to play off the prejudices of the manufacturers and the agriculturists against each other. The import of foreign wool was only taxed from 1819 to 1824, but the amount of the duty, namely, 6d. per lb., was most prejudicial. The government succeeded in persuading the manufacturers, or at least some of them, to consent to the free export of English wool on condition of the free import of foreign wool; and afterwards, with the aid of the manufacturers, they prevented the agricultural interest from re-imposing the duty on foreign wool. But the struggle was a desperate one; and it is humbling to remember that Leeds, Bradford, and Huddersfield were for years on the wrong side. They were happily defeated, and, still more happily, their defeat in this matter made them victors in the next great battle against protection; for there can be no doubt that the liberation of the trade in wool was a step to the liberation of the trade in corn; and thus the great, ugly, and unsafe edifice, miscalled protection, fell story after story, and human industry in all its branches stood upon the same fair level and solid foundation of freedom.

In the working out of this important change, great honour is due to the high intelligence, manly spirit and wonderful disinterestedness of Lord Milton, afterwards Earl Fitzwilliam, who, whilst representing the great seat of the woollen manufacture, Yorkshire, advocated the removal of protection from manufactures, and, although one of the largest landowners, contended for the removal of protection from agriculture. It is a matter of just pride for this Association and for Yorkshire to remember, that that enlightened and high-minded nobleman was the first president of the British Association.

IX.—Distribution of the Woollen Manufacture.

The woollen manufacture in its various branches is very extensively diffused. According to the last factory return, it prevailed in twenty-two counties of England, ten of Wales, twenty-four of Scotland, and six of Ireland. More than one half of the operatives employed in woollen factories are in the county of York; namely, 42,982 out of 79,081. The worsted manufacture, on the other hand, though for some centuries it had its chief seat in Norfolk, Suffolk, and Essex, has now obtained a remarkable concentration in the West Riding of Yorkshire. Of the total factory operatives in the worsted trade of the United Kingdom, there are in Yorkshire 78,994 out of 87,744.

The chief seat of the manufacture of superfine broad cloth has for centuries been, and still is, the West of England, and especially the counties of Gloucester and Wilts. Superfine cloth is made to a considerable extent in Yorkshire, but not equal to the West of England. The manufacturers of this county have always devoted their attention to the middle and lower qualities of woollens; and as these by their cheapness command the most extensive market at home and abroad, whilst by improvements both in the fabric and the finish they come much nearer the finest cloth than formerly, Yorkshire has gained very considerably on Gloucestershire and Wiltshire. This trade illustrates the remarkable tenacity with which particular kinds and modes of manufacture cling to particular localities, almost as if they were fixed by a Hindoo or Egyptian system of caste; and yet also the possibility of overcoming even that tenacity by the revolutionary effect of machinery, and its consequence, cheapness. We see the highest excellence of various manufactures in point of quality in their oldest seats, as of woollens in the west, of worsted goods at Norwich, and of silk in Spitalfields; but these trades have respectively attained a far greater extent and prosperity—the first at Leeds and Huddersfield, the second at Bradford and Halifax, and the third at Manchester and Macclesfield. Superior delicacy and beauty must be accorded to the men of the south; but superior energy and success belong to the rough-spun and rough-spinning men of the north.

The following table shows that the population, and doubtless also the trade, of the West Riding of Yorkshire has increased much more rapidly both in the eighteenth and nineteenth centuries than that of Gloucestershire, Wiltshire, and Norfolk:—

(E.)—POPULATION (PERSONS) OF THE WEST RIDING OF YORKSHIRE, GLOUCESTERSHIRE, WILTSHIRE, AND NORFOLK, IN THE YEARS 1700, 1801, AND 1851.

Counties.	Population in 1700.	Population in 1801.	Population in 1851.	Increase of Population	
				From 1700 to 1801.	From 1801 to 1851.
	Persons.	Persons.	Persons.	Per Cent.	Per Cent.
West Riding of Yorkshire,	242,139	572,168	1,325,495	136	132
Gloucestershire,	157,348	250,723	458,805	59	83
Wiltshire, . .	152,372	183,820	254,221	20	38
Norfolk, . . .	245,842	273,479	442,714	11	62

I apprehend that the principal advantages of the West Riding over Gloucestershire, Wiltshire, and Norfolk consist, first, in the greater cheapness of coal and iron; secondly, in the larger body of men skilled in the making and working of machinery; and thirdly, in the facility of access to the great ports of Liverpool and Hull. But I incline to think that the mere fact of Yorkshire having devoted itself to the manufacture of cheap goods, has been as influential as any other cause.

(F.)—BETWEEN THE YEARS 1801 AND 1851 THE POPULATION OF THE FOLLOWING TOWNS INCREASED THUS :—

Towns.	Population in 1801.	Population in 1851.	Increase.
	Persons.	Persons.	Per Cent.
Leeds, ...	53,161	172,270	224
Bradford, . . .	13,264	103,778	682
Huddersfield, .	7,268	30,880	325
Halifax, . . .	12,010	33,582	179
Norwich, . . .	36,238	68,195	88

X.—Exports of Woollen Goods.

I must now speak of the general statistics of the woollen manufacture, and first of our exports to foreign countries. The earlier tables make no distinction between the woollen and worsted goods exported, and the later tables make the distinction imperfectly. Up to the year 1815 we have only the official value of the exports, which, however, probably did not vary much from the real value; from 1815 downwards we have the real or declared value. Before the year 1820, also, the tables include the exports to Ireland, though this fact is overlooked by most writers on the subject.

The experienced eye will see at a glance how, for the last ninety years, the natural progress of the woollen manufacture has been checked by the introduction of the cheaper material, cotton, and the unparalleled extension of its manufactures, of which, in 1857, we exported to the value of £29,597,316 manufactured goods and £8,691,853 yarn, making a total of £38,289,162.

(G.)—WOOLLEN AND WORSTED GOODS AND YARN EXPORTED, FROM
1718 TO 1785. SELECTED YEARS.

Years.	Manufactured Goods.	Woollen and Worsted Yarn.	Total Woollen & Worsted Exports
	£	£	£
1718 to 1724 ⎱	(Official Value).		(Official Value).
yearly average, ⎰	2,962,000	—	2,962,000
1740	3,056,000	—	3,056,000
1750	4,320,000	—	4,320,000
1760	5,453,000	—	5,453,000
1770	4,113,000	—	4,113,000
1780	2,589,000	—	2,589,000
1790	5,190,000	—	5,190,000
1800	6,917,000	—	6,917,000
1810	5,773,000	—	5,773,000
	(Declared Value).		(Declared Value).
1820	5,586,000	—	5,586,000
1830	4,728,000	122,430	4,851,000
1840	5,327,000	452,000	5,780,000
1850	8,588,000	1,451,000	10,040,000
1857	10,703,000	2,941,000	13,645,000

I next present a table (H), distinguishing, as well as I can, the woollen from the worsted manufactures, and showing the qualities of each description of goods exported, at intervals of ten years, from 1820 to 1857, with the declared value of each description for the year 1857.

It will be remembered that the year 1857 was one of great over-trading, and in 1858 there was a considerable falling off; the value of woollen and worsted goods in that year being £12,731,827. The combined woollen and worsted exports form about one-ninth of the entire export trade of the country. The woollen goods exported were of the value of £4,408,528, the worsted goods £6,294,847; and as the yarn is nearly all worsted, the total worsted exports will be £9,236,647. These figures, of course, do not indicate the respective or proportionate values of the whole production of these two branches of the manufacture of wool, but only of the quantities exported. Including the domestic consumption, there is reason to think that the woollen manufacture somewhat exceeds that of the worsted. But the figures of the following table, especially combined with the considerations mentioned in an earlier part of this paper, would lead to the belief that the worsted manufacture will, ere long, exceed the woollen:—

(H.)—QUANTITIES OF WOOLLEN AND WORSTED GOODS AND YARN EXPORTED, FROM 1820 TO 1857, DISTINGUISHING THE CLASSES OF GOODS; WITH THE DECLARED VALUE FOR 1857.

Descriptions of Goods.	1820.	1830.	1840.	1850.	1857.		Total Declared Value. 1857.
					Quantities	Value.	
						£	£
(I.) WOOLLEN MANUFACTURES.							
Cloth of all kinds, ... pieces.	289,000	388,000	216,000	609,000	695,000	2,956,000	—
Napped Coatings, Duffels, &c. "	60,000	22,000	16,000	3,000	1,000	4,000	—
Kerseymeres, ... "	79,000	35,000	27,000	15,000	4,000	19,000	—
Baizes, ... "	37,000	49,000	35,000	24,000	15,000	51,000	—
Flannel . . . . . . yds.	2,569,000	1,613,000	1,613,000	2,834,000	4,892,000	284,000	—
Blankets and Blanketing. . . "	1,288,000	2,176,000	2,162,000	6,461,000	8,118,000	576,000	—
Hosiery (other than Stockings), val.	—	—	£164,034	£249,757	—	232,000	—
Small Wares (including Rugs), "	—	—			—	91,000	—
Shawls, ... "	—	—			—	195,000	—
Total Woollen Goods,	—	—	—	—	—	—	4,408,000
(II.) WORSTED AND MIXED STUFFS.							
Worsted Stuffs, ... pieces.	828,000	1,252,000	1,718,000	2,122,000	2,568,000	3,325,000	—
Mixed Stuffs — (Worsted, Cotton and Silk), yds.	408,000	1,100,000	3,629,000	52,573,000	57,716,000	2,225,000	—
Carpets and Carpeting, . . "	526,000	673,000	758,000	1,868,000	4,452,000	613,000	—
Stockings, ... doz. pairs.	—	—	97,000	120,000	194,000	130,000	—
Total Worsted Goods, . val.	—	—	—	—	—	—	6,295,000
(III.) WOOLLEN AND WORSTED YARN lbs.	—	1,108,000	3,796,000	13,794,000	23,931,000	2,752,000	—
Woollen and Worsted Yarn, mixed with other Materials "	—	—	—	—	723,000	189,000	—
Total Yarn, ... val.	—	—	—	—	—	—	2,942,000
Total Exports of Woollen and Worsted Goods and Yarn.	—	—	—	—	—	—	13,645,000

XI.—*Persons engaged in the Woollen and Worsted Manufactures.*

In attempting to estimate the entire annual value of the woollen manufacture, I have found difficulties on every side. All the elements for calculating the number of persons employed, and the value of the goods produced, are uncertain and defective. As to the number of persons employed, the census of 1851 makes an approach to the truth, and is the best evidence we have, but it is not altogether trustworthy. The returns of the factory inspectors show the number of operatives in the factories, but not out of them; and, as has been remarked, the number of persons employed out of the factories is proportionably much larger in the woollen than in any other of the textile manufactures. Again, the woollen factories differ so much from each other, that the most careful returns from some of them do not afford safe grounds of calculation for the rest. In some of them there are power-looms or hand-looms, but in two-thirds of the whole there is no weaving carried out. In some the cloth is finished, but in a much greater number it is not finished; whilst about one-seventh of the woollen factories in the return are finishing establishments exclusively. Again, we know the quantity and value of the wool imported, but not of that produced at home, which is doubtless more than the import. We know the amount of manufactured goods exported, but we have no guide to the amount consumed by our own large and flourishing population in these islands. The descriptions of woollen goods are so numerous and diversified, that we cannot average their measurement, their quality, their weight, or their value. It might be supposed that in this, as in other textile manufactures, we might estimate the quantity of wool used and of yarn spun from the number of spindles returned in the woollen factories, and ascertaining the average work per spindle; but unfortunately, according to Mr. Baker, one of the most laborious of the factory inspectors in the collection of statistics, the returns of the woollen spindles are not in the least trustworthy, as some of the inspectors have returned only the billey spindles, which are used in the first stage of spinning, whilst others have returned the mule spindles, used in the second stage. Once more, the woollen manufacture is much more widely diffused over

the United Kingdom than any other manufacture, being found in
sixty-two counties of England, Scotland, and Ireland; owing to
which it is nearly impossible for any private person to gather the
statistics.

Looking at all these difficulties in the way of forming a correct
estimate even now, when we have a census, factory returns, and
many statistical advantages, we cannot be surprised at the loose
and extravagant conjectures formed on the subject before any of
these helps existed, and when the manufacture of wool was the
largest and widest spread department of manufacturing industry.
But the extravagance of those old estimates, copied by writer after
writer, is itself a difficulty in the way of establishing the sober
truth. Towards the close of the last century, it was a prevailing
belief that the woollen and worsted manufactures, directly and
indirectly, engaged 3,000,000 hands. This strange opinion was expressed by Mr. Law (afterwards Lord Ellenborough), as counsel for
the woollen interest at the bar of Parliament in the year 1800, when
opposing the repeal of the prohibition on the export of English wool
to Ireland. So late as the year 1841, in an able article on wool and
its manufactures in the " Encyclopaedia Britannica," the number of
families supported by the manufacture was estimated at 226,298,
comprising 1,218,424 persons. It is extremely difficult to estimate
the number of families, because often the father and several of his
children, and sometimes even the mother, are engaged in different
processes in the same mill; and at other times part of the subsist-
ence of the family may be obtained by an adult or child in one
trade, and the remainder by other members of the family in other
trades. But it is certain that, where so many children are employed,
we cannot consider every worker as the head of a family, and as
supporting four or five others beside himself. Mr. M'Culloch's
knowledge and severe caution induced him to bring down the
estimated number of persons employed in the woollen and worsted
manufactures to 322,000.

The census of 1851 states the number of persons engaged in the
manufactures of wool (that is, both woollen and worsted), in Great
Britain, at 295,276, of whom 125,814 are men, 67,757 women,
50,879 youths, and 50,826 girls.* This includes persons engaged

* Census for 1851.—Ages, Civil Condition, Occupations, &c., vol. i. p. xcv.

in the mercantile trades in wool and woollens, as well as those strictly engaged in the manufacture.

Descending to the particulars comprised within this summary, we find the following items, which I select and arrange, not without doubt in some instances, under the two heads of the Woollen and Worsted Manufactures:—

(I.)—PERSONS ENGAGED IN THE WOOLLEN MANUFACTURE OF GREAT BRITAIN—CENSUS 1851.

	Persons.		Persons.
Woollen cloth manufacturers,	137,814	Wool brokers, agents, 52—divide	
Wool dyers, ...	1,468	with the worsted, ...	26
Wool printers, ...	68	Woollen agents and factors, .	315
Flannel manufacturers, . . .	4,964	" merchants, dealers, .	40
Flannel agents, merchants, . .	56	" drapers, ...	3,799
Fullers, ...	1,469	" flock merchants,	
Baize, listing, serge manu-		dealers, ...	8
facturers, ...	51	" waste dealers, . . .	17
Fancy goods manufacturers		Clothiers, ...	7,308
(?), ...	2,016	Cloth merchants, salesmen—	
Shawl manufacturers (?), . .	5,833	women, ...	761
Wool staplers, merchants,		Felt manufacturers, ...	331
dealers, 2066—divide with		Rag gatherers, dealers (?), . .	3,245
the worsted, ...	1,033	Total, ...	170,622

IN THE WORSTED MANUFACTURE.

	Persons.		Persons.
Worsted manufacturers, . .	104,061	Woollen yarn manufacturers, .	776
Stuff manufacturers, ...	7,500	Worsted dealers, merchants, . .	73
Stuff merchants, ...	20	Wool staplers, merchants, dealers	
Carpet, rug, manufacturers, .	11,457	(half), ...	1,033
		Wool brokers, agents (half), . .	26
		Total, ...	124,946

These two aggregate numbers, of 170,000 in the woollen manufacture and 125,000 in the worsted, make up the whole number assigned by the census to the manufactures of wool, viz., 295,000. Yet, seeing that some of the classes mentioned under the woollen branch are engaged in the mercantile or retail trades, and that others are doubtful, I am disposed to think it would not be safe to take more than 150,000 as actually engaged in the woollen manufacture, whilst probably 125,000 are engaged in the worsted manufacture; making a total in both branches of 275,000. This may also include Ireland, as less than a thousand factory workers are found in the manufactures of wool in that country. The estimate of 150,000 hands for the woollen manufacture is exactly confirmed by an independent computation, founded on the census for the county of York and the factory return of 1856. The census gives 81,221 persons as engaged in the woollen manufacture in this county : the factory return gives 42,982 workers in factories in Yorkshire, and 79,091 in factories in the whole kingdom. If we take the same proportion to exist among the whole of the woollen workers as exists among those in factories, the 81,221 woollen workers in Yorkshire would show the number in the kingdom to be 149,454. Mr. Baker, the factory inspector, considers the number of workers out of the factories to be about the same as those within ; which would give a total of 158,182.

The number of families and individuals supported by the 275,000 persons in the woollen and worsted manufactures, must be to a great degree conjectural. The number, however, must be proportionably larger in the woollen than in the worsted or any other textile manufacture, owing to the larger proportion of men employed. The following are the numbers of the workers employed in the factories of the United Kingdom, with the proportions of adult males : —

(K.)—PERSONS EMPLOYED IN FACTORIES, WITH THE NUMBER AND PROPORTIONS OF MEN.

Class of Factories.	Men Employed.	Total Workers Employed.	Per Centage of Men to all the Workmen.
	No.	No.	Per Cent.
In the cotton factories,	103,882	379,213	27
" woollen factories,	30,672	79,091	39
" worsted factories,	18,079	87,794	21
" flax factories,	13,643	80,262	17
" silk factories,	10,121	56,137	18

But if we take the workers out of the factories, as well as those in them, we shall find a still larger proportion of adult males.

According to the census of 1851, the number of persons employed in the woollen manufacture in the West Riding of Yorkshire was 81,221, of whom 37,519, or 46 per cent. of the whole, were males above twenty years of age.*

I am disposed to think, then, that we may estimate the earnings of each person employed in the woollen manufacture to support three and a half persons, including himself, and in the worsted manufacture two and a half; and at this rate the numbers supported in the respective branches would be as follows:—

(L.)—INDIVIDUAL WORKERS IN THE WOOLLEN AND WORSTED MANUFACTURES, AND ESTIMATED NUMBER OF PERSONS SUPPORTED BY THEM.

Manufacture.	Individual Workers.	Persons Supported.
In the Woollen Manufacture,	150,000 × 3½	525,000
In the Worsted Manufacture,	125,000 × 2½	312,500
Totals, ...	275,000	837,500

It must also be remarked that a larger proportion of persons in auxiliary occupations is connected with the manufactures of wool than with any other textile manufacture, owing to more than one-half of the raw material being raised at home, whilst the cotton and silk are wholly dependent on importation, and the linen almost wholly. According to the calculation of Professor Low, that one shepherd is required for every 600 sheep on the Cheviots, the 35,000,000 sheep supposed to be in these islands would require 58,000 shepherds. There are also, as in connection with the other manufactures, the machine-makers, card-makers, manufacturers of and dealers in dyewares, soap, and oil, persons employed in the conveyance of goods by land and water, those employed in building, and some others.

* Of the 81,221 persons 53,456 were males, and 27,765 females; of the males 37,519 were above twenty years of age, and 15,937 under; of the females 14,420 were above twenty years of age, and 13,345 under.

XII.—*Wages of Operatives in the Woollen Manufacture.*

The wages earned by the operatives in the woollen manufacture are good, and such as must afford the means of comfort to their families, besides indicating a prosperous condition of the trade. I have been favoured with several tables of wages from houses of eminence in the neighbourhood of Leeds, and I have the pleasure to know that they will be received by the statist as of great value. The general return given in Table (M) may be received with entire confidence.

(M.)—AVERAGE WAGES IN THE LEEDS WOOLLEN DISTRICT IN 1858.

Description of Operatives.	Sex, &c.	Wages per Week.
		s. *s.*
Wool Sorters, ...	Men,	24
Wool Scourers, Driers, &c., .	"	16 to 20
Slubbers, ...	"	27
" Overlooker, ...	"	35 to 40
Servers, or Fillers, ...	{ Girls or boys for one } { machine, }	5
" "	For two machines,	9
Billey Piecers, ...	Children,	4s. half-timers 2s.
Cleaners and Willyers, . . .	Young men,	12 to 14
Mule Spinners, ...	Men,	28
" Piecers, ...	Girls or Boys,	6
Warpers, ...	Women,	12
Weavers, Hand-loom, . . .	Men,	15
" Power-loom, . . .	Women,	10 to 12
Overlookers and Tuners, . .	Men,	21 " 28
Knotters, ...	Women,	7 6d.
Burlers, ...	"	5 to 6
Millers, ...	Men,	18 " 20
" Overlooker, ...	"	30 " 40
Dyers, ...	"	16 " 18
" Foreman, ...	"	30 " 60
Dressers, ...	"	20 " 22
"	Young men,	12 " 16
"	Boys,	4 " 9
Dressed Cloth Burlers, . . .	Women,	6 " 7
Drawers, ...	Men,	30 " 40
Tenterers, ...	"	26 " 30
Press Setters, ...	"	35 " 40
Engineman, ...	"	24

The following table (N) is equally deserving of confidence, being from the wage-books of an old and eminent firm. It shows the rate of wages for forty; and in some departments, for more than sixty years.

It will be seen that during the great French war, when the currency was depreciated, food dear, and all prices high, nominal wages were higher than they are now; but that since 1825, notwithstanding a very great abridgment of the hours of labour, wages have remained almost unchanged, whilst both food and clothing have been materially cheapened. It follows that the condition of the operatives must have been considerably improved.

XIII.—*Classes and Proportions of Operatives.*

I add returns of the number of operatives employed in the different departments of two large establishments—one a manufactory of seven billeys, and the other a finishing mill of twenty-four gigs :—

(O.)—LIST OF OPERATIVES EMPLOYED IN A WOOLLEN FACTORY OF 7 BILLEYS (60 SPINDLES TO THE BILLEY).

7 Wool Sorters—Men.
1 Weigher of Wool—Woman.
6 Wool Scourers,Dyers, and
 Driers—Men.

Scribbling Room— 47 hands.
{
7 Slubbers—Men.
1 Overlooker—Man.
4 Cleaners and Willyers—Boys.
21 Billey Piecers—Children.
14 Fillers—Girls or Boys.
}

6 Mule Spinners—Men.
12 " Piecers—Girls or Boys.
4 Warpers—Women.

Weaving Room— 57 hands.
{
50 Power-Loom Weavers—
 Women.
4 Overlookers, Beamers, &c.
 —Men.
3 Tiers in, &c.—Women.
}

33 Knotters and Burlers—
 Women.
4 Millers—Men.
3 Cartmen, Mechanics, &c.—
 Men.

Total ....180 { or 25 to 26 persons per Billey.

"The above calculation supposes that children are used as 'piecers' for the Billey, and one filler for each machine; if, as is generally now the case, piecing machines are used, and 1 female fills 2 machines, the number of hands will be reduced to 21 to 22 per Billey: if 'condensers' are used, the proportion of hands will be nearly the same (viz., 21 to 22), but fewer men and more females or boys will be employed—4 'condensers' being required to do the work of 3 Billeys."

Description of Operatives.	Time of Work.	Piece or Time Work.	1857.	1845.	1835.	1825.	1815.	1805.	1795.
Wool Sorters, men,	7 a.m. to 5.30 p.m.; daylight in winter,	Piece work, average per week	23s. 0d.	22s. 4d. 1844.	26s. 9d. 1833.	29s. 3d. 1827.	37s. 1d. 1816	31s. 1d.	—
Slubbers, men,	60 hours per week, since 1850.	"	27s. 0d.	29s. 6d.	24s. 9d.	26s. 7d.	30s. 6d.	30s. 8d.	22s. 6d.
" foremen.		"	40s. 0d.	40s. 0d.	—	—	—	—	—
Spinners, men,	Do. Any overtime must be worked without piecers.	"	41s. 0d. Deduct 12s.	34s. 11d. for two	37s. 1d. Piecers.	1826. 20s. 4d. Mules introduced & workmen earned at half the price paid to the jenny spinners 40s., less the 12s. to the piecers.	31s. 8d.	24s. 8d.	16s. 9d.
Weavers on power-loom. women,	—	"	12s. 0d.	9s. 0d.	9s. 0d.	—	—	—	—
Millers, men,	62½ hours.	Per week.	18s. to 20s.	—	18s. per wk.	18s. 0d.	18s. 0d.	—	—
" foremen,	"	Per piece.	40s. 0d.	—	30s. "	30s. 0d.	26s. 0d.	—	—
Dyers, men,	58½ hours.	Per week.	16s. to 18s.	16s. to 18s.	16s. to 18s.	16s. to 18s.	—	—	—
" foremen,	"	—	35s. to 60s.	30s. to 70s.	30s. to 70s.	30s. to 40s.	—	—	—
Dressers, men	64½ hours. As boys can only work 60 hours, the men in general only earn this proportion of the full wage.	Per week.	20s. to 21s.	20s. to 21s. 8d.	20s. to 21s.	21s. to 22s.	—	—	—
" young men and boys,		—	6s. to 16s.	5s. to 14s.	5s. to 14s.	4s. to 12s.	—	—	—
" foremen,	—	—	26s. to 30s.	28s. 0d.	28s. 0d.	—	—	—	—

(P.)—LIST OF OPERATIVES EMPLOYED IN A FINISHING MILL WORKING
24 GIGS.

Giggers and Hand-raisers, .	{ 30 Men. / 24 Boys. }	Overlooker for Drawers, &c., .	1 Man.
Cutters, ...	{ 32 Men. / 32 Boys. }	Handle-setters, ... ·	{ 3 Men. / 4 Boys. }
Boilers, ...	{ 2 Men. / 1 Boy. }	List-sewers, ...	4 Women.
Tenterers, ...	6 Men.	Brushers, ... ·	{ 4 Men. / 3 Boys. }
Press-setters, ...	8 Men.	Engineman and Mechanic, .	2 Men.
Burlers, ...	20 Women.	Total, ... 193	{ or 8 / per gig. }
Drawers, ...	17 Women.		

" From statements received from four finishing establishments in Leeds, it appears that their respective averages range from 7 to somewhat over 8 per gig."

The following is a statement of the number of work-people employed, and the weekly wages paid, at one of the largest joint-stock mills in the district, namely, Waterloo Mills, Pudsey, where there is no weaving on the premises, and where the cloth is not finished, but is sold to the Leeds merchants in balk, and finished under their directions in Leeds : —

(Q.)—LIST OF PERSONS EMPLOYED AT WATERLOO MILLS, PUDSEY.
(I.)—ON THE PREMISES.

	Average Weekly Wages each.				Average Weekly Wages each.	
	S.	D.			S.	D.
3 Managers	21	0	14 Piecers for do., above 13 years .		4	0
1 Engine tender, ...	24	0	28 Children, piecers, under 13 years,		2	0
2 Dyers and scourers of wool, . .	25	0	12 Carder fillers, above 13 years . .		5	6
1 Wool dyer, ...	21	0	15 Spinners (with 4920 mule spin-dles), ...		25	0
3 Carriers, ...	15	0				
2 Willyers—one at 14s., one at . .	17	0	15 Piecers for do., above 13 years .		6	0
2 Cleaners or fettlers—one at 13s., one at	14	0	1 Drier of scoured cloth, ...		14	0
			2 Brushers of do.—women, . . .		7	0
3 Young persons teasing, plucking, and moiting wool, above 13 years,	7	0	6 Fullers, ...		22	0
			2 Tenterers, ...		21	0
11 Scribbler fillers—do., ...	7	6	1 Watchman, ...		14	0
12 Slubbers (with 720 billey spindles),	24	0	136			

(II.)—NOT ON THE PREMISES.

			S.	D.
120 Weavers, hand-loom—	Men.	. . . . . .	14	0
7 Warpers, "	Men,	. . . . . .	14	0
40 Burlers, "	Women,	. . . . .	6	0

167

Employed on the premises,	. . . . . .	136
" not on the premises,	. . . . .	167

Total, ... 303

" The wool sorting done by the proprietors themselves.

" The above hands produce about 80 pieces, or 160 ends of cloth, averaging 23 yards per end, or 3680 yards of cloth, weekly. The steam-power employed is about 62 horse."

In this mill, where the cloth is neither woven nor finished, the average earnings of men, women, and children are 11s. 7½d. per week.

In a large manufactory in Leeds, where both manufacturing and finishing are carried on, the following are the wages paid:—

(R.)—WAGES IN A LEEDS WOOLLEN FACTORY, 1858.

		S.	D.		£	S.	D.
200 Men,	averaging	22	3	weekly =	222	10	0
40 Boys,	"	6	8	" =	13	6	8
330 Women and girls,	"	8	0	" =	132	0	0
570 Persons.					367	16	8

Average of the whole, 12s. 11d. weekly.

Here the overlookers are excluded on the one side, and the half-time children on the other, but the latter are only twenty-one in number.

In the flourishing shoddy district, of which Batley is the centre, and where there is finishing as well as manufacturing, the average weekly wage of 5408 operatives is 14s. 1d.

In the dressing establishments of Leeds, according to a return with which I have been favoured by Mr. Baker, inspector of factories, 6175 operatives receive wages averaging 15s. 10d. per week, and those engaged in the manufacture of cloth receive, as at Pudsey, 11s. 7d.

97

G

On the ground of these several facts I feel justified in estimating the wages of operatives in the woollen manufacture at not less than 12s. 6d. per week on the average for men, women, and children; and this for 150,000 workers will give an aggregate of £4,875,000 per annum.

XIV.—The Leeds Clothing District.

Before proceeding to offer an estimate of the total value of the woollen manufacture, I must briefly explain some circumstances relative to the Leeds clothing district, a knowledge of which is necessary to receive that estimate.

Leeds is the ancient seat of the woollen manufacture. Its venerable antiquary and historian, Ralph Thoresby, whose "Ducatus Leodiensis" was published in 1714, declares the town to be " deservedly celebrated both at home and in the most distant trading parts of Europe for the woollen manufacture." He speaks of " the famous cloth market as the life, not of the town alone, but of these parts of England;" and he quotes a record which mentions fulling mills on the river Aire in the forty-sixth of Edward III., the year 1373.

The borough, which of itself had at the last census (1851) a population of 172,270, is the market for a considerable number of clothing villages, the population of which is 104,854—making the aggregate population 277,124, which in the course of the present century has increased 192 per cent.* The district extends on both the banks of the river Aire for about ten miles, touches the towns of Bradford and Otley, and comprises most of the towns and villages between the Aire and the Calder, touching Wakefield, eight miles to the south, and including Dewsbury, Heckmondwike, and Mirfield, nine or ten miles to the south-west, where it borders on the other great woollen district of the West Riding, of which Huddersfield is the centre and market.

The two great woollen districts of the West Riding, Leeds and Huddersfield, are of nearly equal extent: the former is distinguished by the manufacture of broad cloths, and the latter of narrow cloths.

The Leeds clothing district was under the inspectorship of Mr.

* In 1801 the population of the Leeds clothing district was 94,880.

Redgrave, and was divided between two sub-inspectors—Mr. Baker and Mr. Bates. I am indebted to Mr. Baker and Mr. Redgrave for detailed returns of these two divisions, showing (for the year 1856) the number of firms, the horse-power employed, the number of spindles, the power-looms, the gigs, and the operatives of different ages and sexes. The two returns combined give 340 firms, 7810 horse-power, 423,482 spindles, 2344 power-looms, 1005 gigs, and 23,328 factory operatives. This district comprehends something more than one-half of the whole woollen manufacture of Yorkshire; as that of Yorkshire comprehends something more than one-half of the whole woollen manufacture of the United Kingdom. Therefore the Leeds clothing district comprises more than a quarter of the population of the kingdom engaged in this branch of industry, and in this district about 40,000 persons are thus employed.

XV.—*Leeds Cloth Halls and Clothing Villages.*

The manufacturers of the outlying district bring the cloth made in their looms, twice in the week, to be sold to the merchants in the two great cloth halls of this town. It is nearly all in the unfinished state, and is dressed by the Leeds cloth-dressers under the direction of the merchants. The market is held in the forenoon of Tuesday and Saturday, for a single hour on each day—the clothiers standing behind their stands, and the merchants walking between them, examining the goods and making their purchases quickly and silently. After the market the goods are taken to the warehouses of the buyers, measured, and examined more carefully; and the sellers receive payment, purchase their wool, oil, and drysalteries, and return home.

Some years ago it was supposed that the great factories, by the power of capital, the power of machinery, and the saving of time, must entirely destroy the old system of domestic and village manufacture. But they have not materially affected that system. The chief reason has already been explained, in that peculiarity of the woollen fabric which deprives the power-loom of any considerable advantage over the hand-loom. Yet the domestic manufacture must have succumbed, had not the clothiers called machinery to their aid for those processes in which it has an indisputable superiority over hand-labour, that is, in the preparing and spinning. They combined to establish joint-stock mills, where each shareholder takes his own wool, and has it cleaned, dyed, carded, and spun; then, taking the warp or weft to his own house or workshop, he has it woven by the hand-loom, often by members of his own family. The cloth is afterwards fulled at the mill, washed, and tentered; and then, in what is called the balk state, it is conveyed to Leeds and sold, and it is finished by the dressers under the orders of the merchant. Many of these joint-stock mills are well managed, and pay fair dividends to the shareholders. They work by commission for others, as well as for the shareholders. The clothiers, by their industry and frugality, find themselves able to compete with the factory owners, whose great works and complicated machinery entail heavy expenses.

XVI.—The Shoddy Trade.

I must now explain a new branch of the trade, which has risen up with great rapidity and attained extraordinary dimensions—to which, indeed, we are compelled to ascribe much of the present prosperity and extension of the Yorkshire trade. Its origin dates as far back as 1813, but it was long regarded with disapprobation as a dishonest adulteration. It consists in mixing with wool, in the course of manufacture, a very inferior species of wool, made from the tearing up of old woollen and worsted rags, and to which the names have been given of *shoddy* and *mungo*. Shoddy is the produce of soft materials, such as stockings, flannels, &c.; and mungo, of shreds or rags of woollen cloth : the latter is of very superior quality to the former, being generally fine wool, which, after being once manufactured and worn, is torn up into its original fibres (by cylindrical machines armed with teeth), only shorter and feebler, and not susceptible of being dyed a bright colour. Both shoddy and mungo give substance and warmth, and the latter will receive a fine finish; but from the extreme shortness of their fibre the cloth made from them is weak and tender. If cloth made of these kinds of rag-wool is expected to have the tenacity of goods made from new wool, it will utterly disappoint : but there are immense quantities of goods where substance and warmth are the chief requisites, and where strength is of no importance. Among them are paddings, linings, the cloth used for rough and loose great coats, office coats, and even ladies' capes and mantles. Broad cloth may be made with a large admixture of these cheap and inferior materials, to look almost as well as that made of pure wool; but the goods for which they are more properly adapted are what are called pilots, witneys, flushings, friezes, petershams, duffels, honleys, druggets, as well as blankets and carpets.

The price of shoddy varies from ¾d. per lb. to 5d., and the white shoddy from 2d. to 10d. per lb. The average price of mungo is about 5d. per lb. The proportions of these materials used in the Leeds district are about one-third mungo and two-thirds shoddy. Some goods, such as low-coloured blankets and pea-jackets, are made with only one part of pure wool to six parts of shoddy; but, in the whole district, perhaps one-third of wool may be used with two-thirds of shoddy or mungo.

It is one of the objects of improvements in the useful arts to give value to that which possessed no value, to utilize refuse, to economize materials, and, as it were, to prolong their existence under different forms to the latest date. The waste swept up from the floor of the cotton mill is made into beautiful paper. The oil washed out of woollen cloth is now extracted from the muddy liquid which formerly ran to waste, and is saved for fresh oleaginous uses. Scraps, shavings, dust, the contents of sewers, are all made valuable. Why, then, should not the wool of the sheep undergo a second manufacture? If the cloth made of shoddy and mungo is sold for what it really is, no one is deceived. It may, indeed, be fraudulently sold for what it is not, and the man who does so ought to be branded as a cheat. But if the use of shoddy and mungo will answer nearly as well as wool for a vast variety of purposes, and will enable the consumer to obtain two or three yards of cloth where he formerly obtained only one, it should be received as a lawful and valuable improvement in manufacture.

The place where shoddy was first used in this manner was Batley, by Mr. Benjamin Law, and the first machines for tearing up the rags were set up by Messrs. Joseph Jubb and J. & P. Fox. The manufacture has forced its way, and made Batley, Dewsbury, and the neighbourhood, the most prosperous parts of the woollen districts.

There are now in Batley alone fifty rag-machines in thirty-five mills, producing no less than 12,000,000 lbs. of rag-wool per annum (after deducting for loss of weight in the manufacture); and I am assured, on good authority, that three times this quantity is made in the district. The rags are gathered from all parts of the kingdom, as well as imported regularly from the Continent, America, and Australia. There is also now a considerable manufacture of the shoddy, or rag-wool, in Germany, and it is believed that no less than nine or ten million pounds weight was imported last year.

How profitable this trade is to the workmen may be inferred from evidence which has been obtained, to the effect that 5408 operatives in Batley received £3812 of weekly wages, or an average of 14s. 1d. each.

Another method of cheapening cloth has also been extensively introduced in the woollen manufacture, though by no means to the same extent, or with the same success as in the worsted, namely, the use of cotton warps. This also was regarded as a great deterioration of the fabric, and to some extent it is so. The cloth is not so warm as when made all of wool, and it has a certain harshness of feel, but it is not, like shoddy cloth, tender; on the contrary, it is stronger than if made entirely of woollen yarn. Many kinds of goods, of great beauty, are thus made, among which may be mentioned the tweeds used for trowsering, and gray cloths used for ladies' mantles and other purposes. Cloths with cotton warps are generally called Union cloths.

XVII.—Felted Cloth.

There is another branch of the woollen manufacture in Leeds, namely, that of felted cloth, which has arisen within the last few years, and promises considerable extension. It depends wholly on the felting property of wool, and the cloth is made by means of pressure and warm moisture, with milling, and dispenses with the spinning and weaving processes. It is adapted for paddings, carpets, druggets, horse-cloths, table-cloths, and the coverings of boilers, ships' bottoms, &c. Some of the fabrics thus made are handsomely printed in patterns by block-printing. But my limits do not allow me to enlarge on this branch.

XVIII.—*Estimated Annual Value of the Woollen Manufacture.*

In drawing to a conclusion, I must endeavour to estimate the annual value of the woollen manufactures of the kingdom. Uncertain as are several of the important elements in the calculations, I feel considerable confidence, arising out of the abundance of the materials before me, the care with which I have tested them, and the coincidence of several methods of calculation in bringing about nearly the same result. The constituent parts of the value of the woollen goods manufactured in the United Kingdom are—1st, the value of the raw material; 2nd, the value of other articles essential to the manufacture; 3rd, the wages paid to the work-people; and 4th, the sum left to the capitalist for rent, repair, wear and tear of machinery, interest of capital, and profit. My estimate is as follows :—

(S.)—ESTIMATED ANNUAL VALUE OF THE WOOLLEN MANUFACTURE OF THE UNITED KINGDOM, 1858.

(1.) RAW MATERIAL—		Value.
Lbs.		£
75,903,666	Foreign and Colonial Wool, ...	4,717,492
80,000,000	British Wool, at 1s. 3d. per lb., ...	5,080,000
	Shoddy and Mungo—	
45,000,000 {	30,000,000 lbs. Shoddy, at 2½d. per lb., ...	609,370
	15,000,000 lbs. Mungo, at 4¾d. per lb., ...	
	Cotton and Cotton Warps, 1-50th of the Wool, . . .	206,537
200,903,666		10,533,399
(2.) DYE WARES, OIL, AND SOAP, ...		1,500,000
(3.) WAGES—150,000 Work-people, at 12s. 6d. per week, ...		4,875,000
(4.) RENT, Wear and Tear of Machinery, Repairs, Coal, Interest on Capital, and Profit—20 per cent. on the above, ...		3,381,680
TOTAL, ...		£20,290,079

The following explanations may be desirable. The quantity of foreign and colonial wool is that which has been shown to have been left for home consumption, after 15,000,000 lbs. have been deducted for the worsted manufacture—the quantity which Mr.

Forbes, in his lecture on the worsted manufacture before the Society of Arts, and Mr. James, in his laborious and valuable "History of the Worsted Manufacture," assume to be taken. The British wool is one-half of the whole quantity left for consumption, after deducting that exported. The shoddy is below an estimate furnished to me by one of the most experienced and largest dealers in the article, and supported by the judgment of two of the principal manufacturers of Batley. The whole quantity of the raw material, 200,000,000 lbs., is far beyond what I was prepared to expect, or could easily believe; and it is much more than those who are only acquainted with the finer manufacture of the valley of the Aire may at first sight credit. But I was gradually, and by a variety of means, compelled to adopt these figures—first, by finding the enormous amount of low and cheap woollens turned out by the mills of Batley, Dewsbury, and the neighbourhood; secondly, by a computation of the weight and quantity of the goods exported, and taking the proportion which some of our most experienced merchants allege to exist between the exports and the home consumption, and which is three-fourths for home consumption, and one-fourth for export; thirdly, by the separate estimate I have formed of the respective amounts of British wool, foreign and colonial wool, and shoddy; fourthly, by an estimate which the president of the Leeds Chamber of Commerce has formed, and carefully revised, of the value of woollen goods sold in the West Riding; fifthly, by the well-known and often-tested proportion which exists between the cost of the wool and the price of the cloth—the first being nearly fifty per cent. of the second; sixthly, by the proportion which many returns show to exist between the workmen's wages and the value of the goods produced, being about one-fourth on the average.

Now we know the value of wool imported and of woollens exported, on official authority. We know the number of work-people employed, on the authority of the census, supported by the returns of the factory inspectors. We know, from numerous trustworthy returns, the average wages of the work-people. We know something, though imperfectly, of the quantity of machinery and horse-power employed, and of the work which that machinery will turn out. And our large and experienced merchants can judge pretty accurately of the value of goods sold yearly in this district I have had the best assistance which official persons, and our principal manufacturers and merchants, could afford me, and have had the means of checking each by the other. In almost every case I have made an abatement from the information and opinions given me, in order that I might not exaggerate. I should not be justified in now going further into detail; but I offer the facts collected and the conclusions drawn to the multitude of shrewd practical men by whom I am surrounded, as well as to the experienced statists of England.

CHAPTER II.

ALTHOUGH upwards of twelve years have passed since the foregoing account of the woollen trade was written, there is no very important change in the mode in which the woollen manufacture is conducted. There are no machines used now which differ in principle from those used at that period, nor is there any material change in the class of goods produced. It is true that the trade has in many respects undergone great changes, but the change is really a development rather than a fundamental change. These changes, whether referring to the material used, the machinery employed upon it, the class of goods produced from it, and the markets where it is sold, will be noticed under their proper heads.

Although, during the past four years, the woollen trade of the country has not been so prosperous as in the previous eight years, yet on a survey of the period as a whole, it has made very great progress, and may be said to have been as prosperous as any of the great staples of the country; whilst great improvements have been made in nearly all the processes of manufacture, and also in the taste shown in that branch of the trade which consists of figured, or, as they are termed, fancy goods; and new markets have, through treaties with other countries, been opened to a trade which has proved beneficial to both parties.

We will first treat of the material used in pure woollens:—

English wool is but little used for clothing purposes in comparison with the foreign wools. In fact, the principal object of the farmer is to produce a wool longer in the staple than would be desirable to use for woollen cloth. The production of long wool of the best and longest staple is almost confined to this country; and although many attempts have been made by the introduction of English sheep in foreign countries, and also into our own colonies, to produce a wool suitable for common combing purposes, they have not met with much success, and it is found the quality of the wool, as applicable for worsted fabrics, rapidly degenerates. But the worsted trade creates an ample demand for this kind of wool; in fact, notwithstanding the use of cotton warps for stuff goods, the supply has more than once been found inadequate to meet the requirements of the trade, and some five years ago the prices of combing wools reached a point higher than had been the case for near fifty years. Until lately the woollen manufacture only made use of the shorter flocks of the fleece, technically called shorts, and also of the downy part taken out of long wool in the process of combing. Part of such wool was used for cloths, but the great bulk was for blankets, flannels, baizes, &c. But since the introduction of fancy cloths a large trade has sprung up in cloths of a coarse texture, generally of mixed colours, which go by the name of tweeds, as having been principally produced in the south of Scotland, and in the valley of the river Tweed and its tributaries. The production is not, however, confined to that district, but is now found in various parts of England, Scotland, Ireland, and Wales. This trade has greatly increased; and although imported wools are largely used, yet they have competed with the worsted trade for wools which would otherwise have been combed.

No statistics are forthcoming as to the weight of wool produced in this country; but for the past three years returns of the number of sheep in the country have been furnished, and therefore more reliable estimates can be now made than formerly. The quantity will not materially differ from that which was contained in the former account, viz., 150,000,000 lbs.

The woollen trade of this country is principally dependent on foreign wool. Formerly this came from Spain, Germany, and Russia. At the date of the preceding account, the imports of Spanish wool had become very limited, and continue to be so; nor is there any probability that this country will ever again draw any great proportion of the raw material from Spain. The use of German wool continued for some time after that of Spanish was nearly disused; but it, in its turn, has had to give way to the wool produced by our colonial dependencies. There is, however, still a considerable quantity of German wool used, especially for the very finest descriptions of cloth. But the quantity of fine wool imported varies much according to circumstances. When things are in their normal state on the Continent, it is small ; but if anything occurs to disturb the markets and render German wool relatively cheap, our manufacturers and capitalists avail themselves of the opportunity of purchasing them to a greater extent. But with these exceptions the use of German wool remains limited, nor is there any probability that it will increase. A considerable quantity is also imported from Russia, and some of it of very good quality ; the bulk, however, and much of it very inferior, is used for special purposes, and is not generally bought by manufacturers. As in the case of Germany, the quantity varies from year to year ; but in taking an average of several years, it is nearly stationary, and is likely to continue so.

South America, especially the valley of the Plate, has always sent a considerable quantity of wool, and during the past few years it has considerably increased, and is also improving in quality. Large quantities are used for felting purposes ; but it is also valuable for some clothing purposes. From the East Indies, also, a considerable quantity is imported. It is of coarse quality, and is used for druggets, felted carpets, &c.

But the great reliance of the English woollen manufacture for a supply of material, is upon the colonies, especially the Cape of Good Hope, Australia, and New Zealand.

It is of vital importance to a trade, and absolutely necessary to its increase, that it should have a full supply of raw material ; and fortunately the woollen manufacture possesses in our colonies a power of production which seems to have no limit. The statistical tables will show the annual amount imported from them, and will prove that it increases every year. The exact amounts of the Custom House for 1870 are not yet available, but the imports of that year from our Australian colonies reached the enormous amount of 550,000 bales, and from the Cape of Good Hope an additional quantity of 124,473 bales was received. It will be seen that a large quantity of this was exported to the Continent, but the remainder furnished an ample and cheap supply for our own use. The year 1870, owing to the war on the Continent, was an exceptional year ; but in the year 1869 the imports of wool were 255,000,000 lbs., of which nearly 200,000,000 came from Australia and the Cape. The computed value of the whole was upwards of £14,000,000 sterling. About 116,000,000 lbs. was exported, leaving about 140,000,000 lbs. for home consumption, an increase of about sixty per cent. over 1857.

The use of shoddy has greatly extended. This material cannot be produced at will, like wool, cotton, or flax. It is the refuse of wool collected from mill waste, or made from rags, and therefore its quantity depends on the quantity of wool used, and cannot be increased independently of the wool. There has been, however, a great increase in the quantity used, and the increase has been mainly obtained by a more thorough ransacking of every country where woollen rags are to be found. Besides being a utilization of materials which were before almost worthless, and so far a good, its use in moderation is not objectionable ; for many descriptions of cloth a small proportion of it is useful, adding greatly to the beauty and handle of the goods, without injuring its durability in any great degree.

Since 1857 the use of cotton warps has been greatly extended. The high price of cotton consequent on the civil war in the United States was, of course, prejudicial to the trade, but did not interfere with its use so much as might at first be expected. This arises from the fact that the value of the cotton used was much less than that of the wool ; and as there was no corresponding rise in price of the latter, or in wages, a great advance in the price of cotton will only imply a smaller proportionate percentage on the whole.

Of the use of cotton, and also of silk, some account will be given when treating on the classes of goods made during the past few years.

Machinery.—We are not aware of any important invention in woollen machinery during the past thirteen years ; but there have been very great improvements on the machinery then in use. It is better made ; iron has been substituted for wood in the frames and rollers, giving more steadiness ; it works at greater speed, and consequently turns out more work. Many additions which save labour have been made, and the machinery of a well-appointed mill is very different from what it was fourteen years ago. The old billey, which necessitated a breakage of the sliver to be again pieced, is done away with, and the thread comes in one continuous piece from the carder to the other machines, and the slubbing is produced in an unbroken thread ready for the spinner. The thread is therefore much more even, and a comparison of the thread with that of former days shows an immense improvement. It is not unusual to see woollen thread almost as even as doubled cotton.

Self-acting mules have become common; and as existing mules require replacing, self-acting mules will soon become universal.

The hand-loom has long been giving way to the power-loom, and the process is now well nigh complete. Even very small manufacturers now rent a room, or part of a room, in a mill, and sometimes rent the machinery also; and it is not difficult to see that the old domestic manufacture which characterized the woollen more than most other trades, is not far from its end. There is nothing really new in looms, but they are constantly being made better, and to go faster.

Formerly the country was crowded with out-door tenters, on which to dry cloth. These are seen no longer, and machines which stretch and dry the pieces in a very short time are now common, and have proved very effecive.

For the first thirty years of this century, the woollen manufacturer was confined almost altogether to plain cloths and cassimeres generally in self colours, with a few grey mixtures. About 1830 what are called fancy trowserings came into fashion. At first they were of very sober colouring, and merely a bold twill for pattern. In a very few years, however, the variety of design and colouring became much greater and more *prononcée*; but these fancy goods were confined to trowserings, and in Yorkshire the trade was confined to the Huddersfield district. Soon figured woollens began to be used for morning coats as well as for trowsers, and then they were applied to ladies' mantles. The use of these fancy goods for coats gave a heavy blow to the plain cloth trade, in which the west of England and Leeds manufacturers were principally engaged. The plain cloth trade now forms a much less important proportion of the trade than was the case fifteen years ago, and fancy goods are coming more and more into use. During the past few years there has been some revival of the plain cloth trade; but it has only been slight, and is principally owing to the exceptionally low price of

VOL. 1.   4 P

wool during the past two years. In fancy woollens there has been very great improvement during the last fourteen years, especially in the kinds used for ladies' mantles. Formerly this trade was merely a variety of figures, but designs are now commonly made which would then have been deemed impossible, at all events without a very heavy cost. Numerous descriptions of pile have been made, and many kinds of furs are imitated in wool with wonderful success. The use of cotton warp has greatly extended, especially for mantles. The peculiar designs now made, especially when the wool is well thrown up to the surface, enables manufacturers to use a much lower quality of wool, and yet give a softer handle than can be got in plain finished cloth. This and the greater cheapness of cotton warps cause the prices for really handsome goods to be surprisingly low, and has thus brought their use within the means of the poorest. For light summer goods worsted warps are now used, and a considerable quantity of goods of this class are now made. Silk is also used in conjunction with woollen warps, and by putting one or two ounces in the piece, very neat effects are produced.

Plains cloths are now made with cotton warps. They are not likely to supersede the entire woollen cloth for gentlemen's garments; but for some purposes they are equally eligible, and can be afforded at a much lower price.

The use of shoddy has greatly extended. Originally it was used for heavy goods and trowserings, but it is now used for nearly all kinds of woollen fabrics; and though quite unobjectionable, if used judiciously, yet it is to be feared that the character and reputation of our manufacturers is not much increased by it.

There has been a great change in the centres, so to speak, where the merchanting of woollen goods is conducted, especially in Yorkshire. Forty years ago, besides selling the products of their own district, the Leeds merchants bought and sold almost the entire products of the Dewsbury and Batley manufacturers, and above half that of the Huddersfield and Saddleworth districts. There are now many merchants in Huddersfield, and it is probable that they buy from Leeds manufacturers as much as the Leeds merchants buy from those of Huddersfield. A considerable portion of the products of Dewsbury and Batley still go through the hands of Leeds merchants, but a much larger proportion is merchanted by the manufacturers themselves.

There have also been great changes in the foreign markets to which woollens are now exported, part of them, it is to be hoped, from temporary causes, and part, it is equally to be hoped, from causes which will be permanent. Under the first class come the United States. The tariff of the United States has for forty years past been a great bar to the extension of trade between the two countries; but since the civil war it has been still more stringent, and has not only prevented the extension of the trade, but has materially lessened it. Our own colonies also have placed heavy duties on our productions; partly, it is alleged, for revenue, but also, it is to be feared, with a view to protecting and stimulating their own manufactures. In the United States it has been carried to such an extreme by protecting the trades all round, that they are finding that what they gain in higher prices they lose by having to pay higher prices, not only for their own consumption, but also the materials used in their trades. Some little relaxation has been made; and there are signs that still further changes will soon be made, both there and in our own colonies.

About ten years ago the Anglo-French treaty was negotiated, and afterwards treaties were made with the German states constituting the Zollverein, with Belgium, Italy, and Austria. This has led to a considerable trade with these countries, and has been a great boon to the Yorkshire and Scotch woollen manufacturers. Large quantities of foreign woollens are also consumed in this country. This is not on account of lower prices than are demanded by the home manufacturers, at least in most cases; but is on account of the pattern. And under any circumstance this must continue, as there will always be designs invented in one place different to those of another, and for which people who can afford it will pay. At the same time, it cannot be denied that, on the whole, the products of foreign looms are neater and in better taste than the bulk of our own. The distance between the two is, however, by no means so great as it was, and is lessening every year. In speaking of the taste displayed, one point is often forgot: a manufacturer must make goods to suit the taste of the purchaser, and if that is not good, his design must not be good either, or he will lose his trade. In Yorkshire a large portion of the trade is for the million, who must be supplied; and it cannot be expected that their taste will be so refined as that of the classes better educated. This ought always to be considered before blame is cast upon the manufacturers, who would very soon produce goods in better taste, if the demand for them were more general. In low goods, however, colours cannot be produced equal to those in finer goods, and this of itself will always prevent their looking so well.

There has been a considerable advance on wages, so far as the Leeds district is concerned. The work-people have been well employed during almost the whole of the last fourteen years. Certainly the trade has not been so lively since the financial crisis of 1866; but the woollen trade in Leeds has never been really bad, and with very few exceptions, no good workman has been unable to find work for himself and family. The wages are not so high as in some other trades where more skill is required, but they have been as good as ever they were; and in the whole history of the trade there never has been so long a time of equal comfort, if not of absolute prosperity.

There is no exact division of particular branches of the trade in the several woollen districts, but the following is perhaps as nearly correct as can be:—

In the West of England, the largest quantity of superfine plain broad cloths are made; also fine fancy trowserings and fine coatings. In the Leeds district, a considerable quantity of first class plain broad cloths are made; also plain cloths with cotton warps, now a large business, and nearly confined to the Leeds district; also some fine fancy coatings; immense quantities of lower fancy coatings, both all wool and with cotton warps; fancy cloths for ladies wear, a species of light cloth called Spanish stripes, because they have striped lists. These are dyed scarlet, yellow, light blue and other showy colours, and are largely exported to China and Japan. Army cloths and carriage cloths are also largely manufactured. In the Dewsbury and Batley districts very heavy goods for great coats and mantles are principally made; as pilots, beavers, presidents, &c., also army cloths. In the Huddersfield district are made some fine cloths, and some fancy coatings; but the principal branch is in fancy trowserings of all classes and qualities. Old-fashioned strong and heavy goods, as cassimeres, are still made, and also heavy cloths

113

H

for coachmen's great-coats and liveries. In Heckmondwike and Earlsheaton large quantities of blankets are made. Saddleworth once had a very large number of small manufacturers, who made fine cloths; there are some left, but practically Saddleworth is now out of the woollen district. All-wool tweeds, which are unfinished, coarse-looking, and resembling in many respects the fabrics which would be made by farmers, when every well-to-do family spun its own clothing, are made principally in the south of Scotland, Dumfriesshire, Bannockburn, near Stirling, and in Aberdeen. Similar goods are also made in several parts of England, also in Ireland, and some in Wales. Flannels are principally made in the neighbourhood of Rochdale, and in many parts of North Wales, especially in Montgomeryshire.

Wages are very variable. In districts where the men are well employed in other trades, the children and women work for lower wages, and mills are often built in such places on that account, though disadvantageous in other respects; as price of coal, distance from market, &c., &c. These, on the whole, may be said as a rule to be a fair set-off against the low wages; but, on the other hand, if the mills were all in the most suitable places in all other respects than wages, a sufficient number of hands could not be had. On the whole, wages have advanced in the Leeds district about ten to fifteen per cent. since 1856.

WOOLLEN FACTORIES IN THE UNITED KINGDOM IN 1870.

No. of Factories. 1939.	No. of Spindles. 2,690,000.	No. of Looms. 48,140.	Moving Power; Horses. 52,302.	Persons Employed. 125,130.

CLOTH DRESSING.

CLASS OF OPERATIVE.	Leeds.			
	s. d.	s. d.	s. d.	
Giggers, ...	—	—	23 0	
Giggers, ...	—	—	18 0	
Machinists, ...	—	—	23 0	
Machinists, Perpetual, ...	10 0	14 0	23 0	
Cloth pressers, ...	—	—	35 0	Paid by the piece.
Cloth drawers, ...	—	—	35 0	" "
Cloth tenterers, ...	—	—	28 0	" "
Handle setters, ...	—	—	30 0	" "
Handraisers, ...	—	16 0	22 0	" "
Foremen, ...	—	33 0	35 0	

AVERAGE EARNINGS OF OPERATIVES ENGAGED IN THE WOOLLEN
MANUFACTURE—SPINNING, WEAVING, &C.

CLASS OF OPERATIVE.	Rochdale.	Dews-bury.	Leeds.	Man-chester.	Neighbourhood of Dewsbury.	Neighbourhood of Huddersfield.
	s. d. s. d.	s. d.	s. d.	s. d.	s. d. s. d.	s. d. s. d.
Layers on for scribblers, women,	12 0	12 0	9 0	—	10 0 to 12 0	7 6
Card setters or cleaners, men,	18 0 to 20 0	17 0	—	17 0	19 0	—
Sliver minders, girls,	—	—	9 0	—	—	—
Condenser minders, girls,	—	10 0	7 0	—	—	—
Card feeders, women,	10 0 to 12 0	—	—	13 0	—	—
Woollyers, men,	15 0	16 0	20 0	17 0	10 0 to 16 0	18 0
Woollyers foremen, men,	20 0	21 0	—	—	—	—
Self-acting mule minders, men,	18 0 to 23 0	15 0	—	12 0	—	—
Self-acting mule piecers, boys,	7 0	7 0	6 0	5 0	—	—
Self-acting mule-piecers, boys and girls, half-timers,	2 6 to 3 6	—	—	—	—	—
Rag grinders, men,	—	—	20 0	—	—	—
Enginemen and firers up, or stokers,	19 0 to 21 0	20 0	—	—	—	—
Warpers,	15 0 to 18 0	15 0	—	14 0	12 0 to 18 0	—
Power loom tuners, men,	24 0	35 0	—	—	24 0 to 50 0	24 0
Power loom weavers, women,	14 0	14 0	12 0	14 0	10 0 to 16 0	11 0 to 16 0
Wool sorters, men,	26 0	25 0	25 0	—	18 0 to 23 0	22 0 to 26 0
Fulling millers, men,	23 6	21 0	—	22 0	25 0 to 35 0	20 0 to 21 0
Wool and piece dyers, men,	—	22 0	—	—	—	18 0
Cloth dressers, viz., raisers, cutters, pressers, tenterers, drawers,	—	24 0	22 0	21 0	—	20 0
Burlers, women,	9 0	10 0	5 0	—	9 0 to 12 0	8 0 to 9 0
Jiggers and stumpers, men,	—	21 0	—	—	—	—
Fenders and stumpers, women,	—	13 0	—	—	—	—
Oil extractors, men,	—	24 0	—	—	—	18 0
Mechanics and joiners, men,	27 0	30 0	—	—	18 0 to 30 0	27 0
Rag pickers, women,	—	8 0	—	—	—	—
Hand spinners, men,	22 0	28 0	—	—	25 0 to 30 0	24 0 to 30 0
Hand spinners, young persons,	—	—	—	—	—	6 0
Rubbers,	22 0 to 23 0	26 0	—	—	—	27 0

CARPET MAKING.

Class of Operative.	Glasgow. s. d.	Kilmarnock. s. d.	Durham.	Neighbourhood of Leeds.
Assistant dyers, men,	18 6	—	16 0 to 30 0	16 0 to 18 0
Assistant dyers, boys,	6 4	—	6 0 to 14 0	10 0 to 14 0
Hand-loom weavers and beamers, men,	20 6	20 0	22s.	18 0 to 25 0
Hand-loom weavers and beamers, boys,	8 0	—	14s.	12 0 to 18 0
Mechanics,	26 0	—	26 0 to 32 0	—
Pattern drawers, men,	25 0	—	—	—
Pattern drawers, boys,	10 0	—	—	—
Warehouse workers, tenters, and sewers, men,	22 0	—	—	—
Warehouse workers, tenters, and sewers, boys,	6 0	—	—	—
Warehouse workers, tenters, and sewers, women,	9 9	—	—	—
Warehouse workers, tenters, and sewers, girls,	7 0	—	—	—
Croppers, cutters, and cleaners, men,	19 0	—	—	—
Croppers, cutters, and cleaners, boys,	7 0	—	—	—
Croppers, cutters, and cleaners, women,	9 0	—	—	—
Croppers, cutters, and cleaners, girls,	4 6	—	—	—
Winders and reelers, women,	9 0	5 0	6 4 to 7 10	10s.
Winders and reelers, girls,	5 0	23 0	—	—
Power-loom weavers, Brussels carpets, men,	—	—	26s.	30s.
Power-loom weavers, Brussels carpets, apprentices,	—	—	18s.	12s.
Carding and spinning, men,	—	—	17 6 to 32 0	—
Carding and spinning, lads,	—	—	4 0 to 10 0	—
Carding and spinning, females and children,	—	—	3 6 to 10 0	—
Carders, females,	—	6 6	—	11s.
Spinners, females,	—	5 0	—	—

FOREIGN AND COLONIAL WOOL IMPORTED AND EXPORTED IN LBS.

Years.	Imports. Lbs.	Exports. Lbs.
1858	126,738,723	26,701,542
1859	133,284,634	29,106,750
1860	148,396,577	30,761,867
1861	147,172,841	54,377,104
1862	171,943,472	48,076,499
1863	177,377,664	63,932,929
1864	206,473,045	55,933,739
1865	212,206,747	82,444,930
1866	239,358,689	66,573,488
1867	283,703,184	90,832,584
1868	252,744,155	105,070,311
1869	258,461,589	116,608,305
1870	263,250,499	92,542,384

EXPORTS OF WOOLLEN YARNS, WORSTED, AND WOOLLEN MANUFACTURES IN VALUE.

	1860.	1865.	1866.	1867.	1868.	1869.	1870.
	£	£	£	£	£	£	£
Wool, Sheep and Lambs'	877,082	901,660	895,356	775,834	736,035	922,656	575,583
Woollen and Worsted Yarn,	3,843,450	5,429,504	4,742,162	5,822,996	6,364,011	5,857,905	5,175,757
Woollen and Worsted Manufactures:—							
Cloths, Coatings, &c., Unmixed and Mixed,	2,996,091	4,023,954	5,303,602	5,327,375	3,760,961	4,272,949	4,740,369
Flannels, Blankets, Blanketing, and Baizes,	848,186	1,203,127	1,161,615	859,519	963,866	1,107,360	1,098,828
Worsted Stuffs, Unmixed and Mixed,	7,012,793	13,360,527	13,294,059	12,144,998	13,075,773	15,119,029	13,797,738
Carpets and Druggets,	667,370	861,453	1,217,682	1,101,986	1,099,882	1,467,355	1,393,576
all other Sorts, . .	632,558	655,669	819,259	687,054	635,591	658,497	619,949
Total of Woollen and Worsted Manufac.,	12,156,998	20,104,730	21,796,217	20,120,932	19,536,073	22,625,190	21,650,460

117

CHAPTER III.

THE WORSTED TRADE.

A LARGE county like Yorkshire, with its 3,923,697 statute acres of mountain, plain, and valley, and its population of upwards of 2,000,000, must be the home of many and diverse industries. In the North and East Ridings agriculture yet occupies the foremost place, though other forms of labour are rapidly rising into prominence, as is iron in Cleveland and Middlesborough, and ancient methods still retain their life, as does lead mining in Arkendale. The West Riding, larger and much more densely populated, while not neglecting the cultivation of the soil, has turned its energies in the direction of manufacturing and mercantile activities. Notable amongst them, and indeed amongst those of the first importance in England, is the worsted manufacture, the growth of which it is proposed to trace in this paper. In the brief space which alone can be afforded in these volumes for such a task, little more than a rapid outline can be given. Those who desire to understand its details must refer to some comprehensive work, like that of Mr. John James, whose " History of the Worsted Trade " is, for the time it covers, a complete text-book on the subject.

Worsted is defined, dictionary-wise, as " yarn spun from combed wool," but this scarcely conveys to the general reader a clear notion of what it means. We shall go a little more into particulars. In every fleece of wool there are two kinds of hair, distinguished as " long " and " short." The long wool is separated from the rest, and drawn out by " combing " into straight and even lengths. This long wool, so combed, was the original " worsted," and it is yet the main basis of the worsted fabric. The short wool, instead of being combed out into lengths, is valued for its capacity of coiling and " felting together," and goes to the production of woollen cloth. But the

VOL. 1.   4 Q word " worsted " has lately been much extended in its meaning. So many substances besides combed wool have come to be used in the goods manufactured in the worsted district, while the word itself has remained unchanged, that its original signification has altogether ceased to apply. Cotton and silk warps, alpaca, mohair, china grass, &c. (the two former especially), have become so uniformly constituent parts of what are called worsted pieces, that the word must now be held to cover any kind of piece in which combed wool is employed.

Though it is not true, as some writers have supposed, that Edward III. was the originator in England of the woollen and worsted manufactures, it is true that before his time they were comparatively unimportant, and that he gave a great impetus to their progress. He invited a great number of Flemish weavers to settle in this country. They chose Norfolk, Sussex, and Essex as their resting-places, and Norwich became the chief centre of their industry, a distinction which it retained for nearly five centuries. They probably improved the trade; they certainly largely extended it. The king and his queen, Philippa, who was bound to the immigrants by the tie of nationality, often visited Norwich, and bestowed upon it many marks of honour, one of which (the establishment of the king's staple there) gave, it is said, great offence to its neighbour Yarmouth. But it was not at once that they proceeded to manufacture the finer cloths. A curious tract, " The Circle of Commerce," published in 1623, reveals the fact that, while the value of the cloths exported by the manufacturers in England was only, on the average, 40s. the piece, the average value of imported pieces was £6.

The English people do not appear to have taken kindly to the foreigners. They broke the looms, and in some cases the limbs, of the poachers upon their manor; committing such and so many outrages, indeed, that the king was compelled to issue special letters of protection in behalf of the strangers. It was not until the end of the reign of Henry IV. that a better feeling began to prevail. Perhaps they had learnt to see the evils which the quarrel had brought upon their trade, and in the beginning of the fifteenth century the English portion of the Norwich weavers petitioned that the alien workmen might be incorporated into the English guild.

A further immigration of Flemish manufacturers was invited by

119

Henry VII., in whose reign the woollen and worsted trades, which in the troublous times that preceded his accession and marriage had greatly decayed, were much extended and strengthened. It is clear that much difficulty was experienced in dealing with the frauds of the manufacturers, who made "untrue wares of all manner of worsted," not only in size but in material, and that serious damage to the trade had grown out of their malpractices. It was the expressed opinion of the Norwich people, that another cause was equally efficacious for evil. A law had been passed in the seventh year of the reign of Henry IV., at the instance and for the protection of Norwich, which provided that "no man or woman should put their son or daughter to be an apprentice" in a city or town, unless they had "lands or rents to the value of twenty shillings at least by the year." This fortunate class was only a small fraction of the whole, and utterly unable to furnish a sufficient number of apprentices to keep the trade going; while those who were excluded fell into ruinous "idleness, vice, and other misgovernances," which threatened the destruction of the city. Now, under Henry VII., these protectors of existing industry saw the error they had committed, and prayed for the removal of the restrictions they had previously demanded. Their request was complied with, first in the city of Norwich, and one year afterwards throughout the whole county of Norfolk, and the weaving trade recovered its vigour and elasticity. Under Henry VIII. a reaction occurred again, arising mainly, as it would appear, from the fraudulent practices of those who were in the trade. Parliament stepped in to the rescue, and passed an Act to extirpate "deceit in worsteds." It is to be feared that this object was never thoroughly accomplished, if we may judge from trading phenomena which are yet unfortunately too common. A remedy was sought in the prohibition of the export of English wool to foreign countries, but as the foreign manufacturer would have it, the prohibition only acted as an incentive to smuggling. Towards the close of the reign this distress greatly increased. Wool became scarce and dear, and the consequent conversion of farms into sheep-walks seriously interfered with the accustomed course of husbandry. The small spinners were forbidden to purchase wool for their own use, the monopoly of the trade being reserved for merchants of the staple and manufacturers. Add to these causes of discontent and

disaster, a new immigration of Protestant weavers from the Nether-
lands, and the disarrangement of society caused by the suppression
of the religious houses—Norwich alone had sixty parish and seven
conventual churches within its walls—and we can scarcely wonder
that dissatisfaction became nearly universal, or that it broke out, in
1549, into open revolt.

Under Elizabeth began a new period of prosperity. The cruelty
of the duke of Alva drove large numbers of Flemish and Dutch
weavers into exile. Many came to England. The inhabitants of
Norwich, which had greatly decayed, petitioned the queen that a
certain number might settle in their city, and she granted permission
to thirty master workmen, each of whom was to be allowed ten
assistants. Their energy gave renewed life to the trade, and from
300 the foreigners increased to 4000. The queen herself visited
Norwich, and had a magnificent reception, the foreign artizans in
particular exhibiting a pageant illustrative of all the principal
processes in their art. The impetus which they gave to the worsted
manufacture was not so much by the introduction of new stuffs, as
by the greater rapidity and increased variety of their productions.
But from this time it must be counted amongst the most extensive
and important industries of the realm. Colchester and Canterbury
began to make the fine worsteds, and the latter place deservedly
acquired high reputation.

Between 1743 and 1763 Norwich, it has been said, was "the chief
seat of the chief manufacture of the realm." Its merchants carried
on a large and flourishing export trade "with Holland, Flanders,
Germany, Italy, Spain, and Portugal, and through them with the
great markets of South America." But its progress was arrested by
the outbreak of the American war of Independence, the system of
privateering practically banishing its commerce from the seas.
Meanwhile, towards the end of the eighteenth century, the bulk of
the trade was being rapidly concentrated in the north. Amongst
other places, Kilmarnock, Stirling, and Aberdeen drove a thriving
trade, but it was not in Scotland that the manufacture was destined
to achieve its greatest successes. The natural advantages of Yorkshire for manufacturing purposes are far greater than those of the
eastern counties. Water, coal, and iron abound, and the people of
the great shire have a special reputation, based on solid reasons, for

industry and untiring perseverance. Notices of the existence of the trade in Yorkshire appear in the time of Henry VIII., York itself being notable for the manufacture of stout worsted coverlets, which includes all the processes of spinning, dyeing, carding, and weaving. About the beginning of the eighteenth century it began to vary, here and there, the general industry of cloth weaving, Bradford and Halifax being among the earliest seats of the new business. By 1750 these two towns were actually engaged in it, and Leeds, the woollen cloth metropolis, contrived to manufacture a considerable quantity of worsteds. In 1772 the value of the trade in the West Riding was estimated, for Parliament, at £1,404,000, as against £1,200,000 in Norfolk and adjacent districts.

As the manufacture grew, employers began to suffer from frauds on the part of their workpeople : woolcombers embezzled the wool intrusted to them, spinners reeled false or short yarn, and a system of terrorism and combination prevented individual employers from enforcing the law. Ultimately the manufactures of Yorkshire, Lancashire, and Cheshire convinced Parliament of the necessity of special legislation in the matter, and the "Worsted Acts" were passed in 1777. These Acts authorized the establishment of a committee, which was to watch over and protect the interests of the trade, and bring delinquents to justice. Their provisions were very stringent; in some respects indeed they violated, and still violate, the recognized principles of English law, but they have been administered in the main with fairness, and they have certainly almost extinguished the evils they were designed to repress. The worsted committee was not always content, in earlier times at least, to restrict its efforts to the prevention of fraud. It fought ardently, for instance, against the use of machinery, and afterwards, with equal ardour, against the exportation of machinery; and it has generally defended the fallacious doctrine of protection to native industry which a wiser political economy has exploded. Yet, on the whole, its administration has been beneficial to the trade whose conduct and regulations it was appointed to control.

In 1780 the Lincoln wool-growers, pressed by falling prices and stagnant trade, sought for power to export their long wools. Vigorous resistance was instituted by York and Norfolk, in which Exeter speedily joined. In vain the Lincoln men maintained " that, after a certain period subsequent to the clipping, the long and coarse wools which could not be sold at home ought in justice to be allowed sale in the foreign markets." Neither the nation nor the senate would listen to the proposition. On the contrary, the growers had to submit, a few years later, to more rigorous legislation than ever against the exportation of wool, the penalties imposed by the Act 28 Geo. III. cap. 38, including fines, solitary imprisonment, and forfeiture of ship and cargo.

In 1782 the American war was ended and trade renewed its life. Yarn became scanty, and the Yorkshire dales grew unable to supply the needs of the manufacturers. Recourse was had to Norfolk, Sussex, and Essex, which now began to supply yarn for the northern traders to work up. The entire force of hand-spinners became totally inadequate at last, and machine-spinning, which had for years been applied to cotton, was in 1784 adopted for wool at Dolphin-Holme, on the Wyre. The first spinning works were rude enough, and, pioneer-like, were unsuccessful. Addingham, Hewnden, and Mytholmroyd followed, and at last, in 1794, Bradford.

It is not very easy, nor perhaps very important, to determine in what order the different worsted fabrics began to be manufactured in the West Riding. A general estimate of the Yorkshire woollen manufacture, prepared in 1772 by Mr. Wolrich of Leeds, includes the names of " shalloons, calimancoes, Russells, tammies, single camblets or camblettees, prunells, and moreens, all made of single yarns; everlastings, figured and flowered Amiens, serges de Nismes, and serges de Rome, whose warps are of double yarn." Later on we find the names of wildbores, Waterloos, dobbies. Later still, we have damasks, French merinos, merinos, full twills, French figures, alpaca figures, figured Orleans, and the hundred other varieties known to the present day.

The progress of the trade necessitated corresponding improvements in the buildings where its manufacturers and merchants were to meet. In 1766 the Tammy Hall at Wakefield was erected. Bradford Piece Hall was founded in 1773. The Piece Hall at Colne was built in 1775. Halifax reared its Manufacturers' Hall in 1779, and Huddersfield, Keighley, and Bingley were all actively engaged in the spinning and weaving of worsted, although the inhabitants of those towns did not follow their enterprising neighbours so far as to build market houses.

Up to about 1800 the trade in the north was scattered over a considerable district in Airedale and Calderdale, and just across the border into Lancashire, Halifax taking the first position for the activity, importance, and enterprise of its traders. From that period dates the rapid rise of Bradford into pre-eminence, first in the north of England, and now throughout the world, so far as respects this branch of industry. The original superiority of Halifax died with the French war. Its manufacturers and merchants shrank from encountering the risks and losses attendant upon foreign trade with continental markets closed. As they withdrew from business altogether, or embarked in the cotton trade, and as the Norwich people, from want of energy or want of foresight, omitted to avail themselves of the machinery which the northern town was utilizing as far as possible, Bradford soon took the undisputed lead. In 1810 the drawback on soap used by manufacturers of combing wool in Bradford was more than double the amount allowed in any other part of the worsted district. Shortly afterwards, about 1812, Halifax introduced into Yorkshire the manufacture of moreens, which up to that time had been peculiar to Norwich, and Messrs. Akroyd of Halifax, in 1813 and 1814, began to produce "plainbacks" and "wildbores," the forerunners of single-twilled merinos. In 1819 the same firm manufactured Norwich crape. After a period of depression, which had extended over nearly four years, an enormous increase of the trade took place in 1818. Nearly 25,000,000 lbs. of wool, almost double the importation of the preceding year, were brought from abroad, and the number of pieces exported increased from 683,000 to 938,000. In the same year great improvements were made in the methods of preparing and spinning worsted yarns, which made it possible to obtain better qualities of warp and weft from the same quality of wool.

In the year 1825 the law prohibiting the exportation of British wool was repealed, and English manufacturers, driven to compete with those of France, still further improved their processes, with the result of producing "merinos and other stuffs in every respect equal" to French goods. The year 1825 is memorable also for a prolonged strike among the wool-combers, whose weekly wages were then, on the average, 23s., for an advance of wages in the

Bradford district. Twenty thousand combers and weavers were out of employment for twenty-two weeks, and were compelled to resume work without gaining their object. Their own sufferings and privations were terribly severe, and the money loss of the employers was immense. There is only one relief to the sadness of the picture. Not a single outrage or breach of the peace appears to have been committed from beginning to end of the contest. Worse consequences followed the introduction of the power-loom. In 1826 a number of hand-loom weavers attacked the mill of Messrs. Horsfall, of Bradford, who first employed the new loom; and a sharp conflict between special constables and the mob ended in the death of two persons, the wounding of many, and the ultimate punishment of numbers who took part in the outbreak. There have been many strikes since, local and limited, but physical conflict has always been avoided.

The changes in the processes of the worsted industry necessarily led for a time to much suffering amongst the classes displaced. Great distress was endured by the hand-loom weavers when their shuttles were silenced by the surer and swifter energy of steam; and the condition of the wool-combers, after the extinction of their trade by the introduction of machine-combing, would supply material for one of the most melancholy chapters of Yorkshire history. In course of time the workers who were put aside found other means of gaining a livelihood, in some cases at home, in others abroad, but much and sad privation had to be undergone before relief was felt. Occasional periods of exceptional depression of trade, happening probably about once in ten years, have caused considerable loss to employers, and suffering to employed, by the enforced cessation of labour; but these have never come near, either in intensity or extent, to the great crisis brought about by the substitution of steam for hand-labour in the processes of weaving and combing.

Our space is too limited to permit us to trace, in anything beyond the merest outline, the history of the inventions which have rendered possible the enormous development of the worsted manufacture. Yet, between the distaff and spindle of the ancients, and the wonderful process by which wool is now converted into yarn, separated as they are by vast differences both in method and result, there is a connection of growth and affiliation not only interesting in itself, but essential to be understood by all who intend to possess a definite idea of the subject. That process of development we propose to relate as succinctly as may be, consistently with clearness. We must necessarily pass over many details, but we shall endeavour to preserve every feature of importance.

Hand-spinning may be taken as the starting point of the narrative. The Norfolk spinners, in the early times, dispensed even with the wheel, making their primitive yarn by a dexterous and patient twisting of the threads with the hand upon the thigh, unquestionably the most primitive of all spindles. Then came the one-thread wheel, an immense advance, which set the hands free to draw out the thread, and largely increased the quantity of yarn produced. The Saxon wheel, in use a century and a half or two centuries ago, marks a still further point attained in the communication of the necessary twist to the yarn, by a flier "revolving with greater rapidity than the bobbin" on which the thread was wound. These contrivances represent the measure of progress attained in the art of spinning, up to about the year 1738, when the germ principle of the modern spinning frame appears to have been hit upon by John Wyatt, who first, at Sutton Coldfield in Warwickshire, appears to have spun thread by means of rollers. His system was put in action in 1741 at Birmingham, not with the modern aids of water and steam power, but worked by a gin, which was turned by two asses, and attended by ten girls. Poor Wyatt, like many of his race, fell into the hands of speculators; became unfortunate, was confined for debt, and ultimately died in poverty. His little manufactory was closed, as also was, about 1764, another which had been worked at Northampton on Wyatt's principle by water-power, and for a while the invention slept. About 1769 James Hargreaves, an uncultured but ingenious weaver who lived near Church, in Lancashire, invented the spinning jenny, which at last he so improved as to work eighty spindles, having begun originally with eight. All prior inventions, however, were destined to yield to those of Richard Arkwright, whose primary purpose of searching after "perpetual motion" ended, in 1769, in his patenting a machine "for the making of weft or yarn from cotton flax or wool," which revolutionized the history

VOL 1.   4 R of manufactures in England. It greatly improved the quality of the yarn produced, and immensely increased its quantity, while it laid the foundation of the factory system by rendering associated labour a necessity. The prior habit of solitary spinning at home, varied only by the gossiping friendliness of half a dozen chattering spinsters, working together towards sunset in the village street, was marked for extinction sooner or later, from the hour when Arkwright's invention gave a celerity and precision to the art which the human hand could never hope to rival. Next, about 1780 or shortly after, Samuel Crompton's ingenious device to combine the jenny spinning of Hargreaves with the roller spinning of Arkwright produced the hand mule, which still retains its superiority for fine yarns, and which, in the production of fineness and equality in the yarn, surpassed the machines of all preceding inventors. The limit of fineness reached by that of Arkwright (the best till then) was eighty hanks of cotton to the pound; by the hand mule no less than 120 hanks could be spun, and of a more equal texture. Further improvements have carried this fineness so far, that 300 to 500 hanks of 840 yards each are now manufactured to the pound for trade use; and once at least, as an exhibition *tour de force*, a pound of cotton has been spun to 2150 hanks, or upwards of 1000 miles in length. The self-acting mule, invented by Mr. Roberts, of Manchester, seems to have carried the principle of automatic labour to its utmost development, the machine itself doing the whole of the spinning work, and the duty of the attendant being reduced to the simple task of joining threads which have become accidentally broken. Worsted yarns are invariably spun on frames which combine the roller drawing with the spindle and fly, or a modification of it in the cap frame, while the spinning of woollen or uncombed yarn is generally accomplished by the mule. As a rule, worsted yarns seldom exceed in fineness 100 hanks of 560 yards each to the pound.

The greatest impetus to the textile manufactures was, however, given, about eighty years ago, by the application of steam-power to the processes employed. The inventions of Sir Richard Arkwright would have remained of comparatively small importance, had not the genius of James Watt devised the means of multiplying human power to an inconceivable extent by setting steam to do its manual

127

work. Steam-power was not applied to the worsted manufacture until the early years of the present century. Vaucanson, in 1765, had invented a weaving loom, which was tried in Manchester, but ultimately came to nothing. Dr. Cartwright was more successful for a time, but there were essential imperfections in his loom which prevented its coming into general use. Others tried their skill at improvement with more or less success, but it was reserved for Mr. Horrox, of Stockport, to carry Cartwright's idea into really practicable shape. To him it is that we owe the "crank power-loom" now in common use, and later inventors have been content to aim at improvement in details, rather than alteration in principles. The Jacquard loom was first used in the worsted manufacture, about 1827, by Mr. James Akroyd, junr., of Halifax. In a few years it was generally adopted, and its employment gave an immense development to the trade in figured goods.

Steam and machinery, indeed, have now superseded hand labour in every department of the worsted manufacture. For a long time, the combing of wool by machinery defied the utmost efforts of inventors, and it is only within the present generation that they have succeeded. It was attempted in 1790 by Dr. Cartwright, with his usual ability; but like most first attempts, the machinery was rude, and under the combined weight of its own imperfections and the storm of opposition it aroused from those who thought their interests threatened by its introduction, the project fell to the ground. Peatt and Colliers, in 1827, patented another method, which was superseded in 1846 by the greatly improved machinery of Heilmann. This was again improved upon by Mr. Donisthorpe, Mr. Samuel Cunliffe Lister, and Mr. Isaac Holden, of Bradford, who, above all others, are entitled to the credit of having mastered the problem. To the invention and enterprise of Mr. Holden, more particularly, may be ascribed the present perfection of wool-combing machinery.* Other machines have contributed towards the great ends of simplicity and use, and the net result is a vast advance over the old arrangements. Under the old process of hand-combing, which was at once rude and wasteful, a considerable length of staple was required, and much was lost in consequence of the

* His immense establishments in England and France are unquestionably the largest, the busiest, and the most efficient for their purpose in existence.

"coiling" of the fibres; but the exquisite machines now in use are able to comb any kind of English wool from three-inch staple upwards, and as nearly as possible without waste.

For a long time the northern manufacturers confined themselves to rapidity and extent of production, neglecting the essential art of design. They were consequently greatly distanced by other districts and other countries, where the inhabitants were wiser in their generation. Their materials and their combinations were good, but the taste which was needful to make them compete in attractiveness with the productions of rival looms was absent. The remedy soon followed the perception of the defect. Schools of design were established about twenty years ago. They were attended with considerable success, and their effects were speedily seen in the new grace and beauty of the fabrics produced. The critical jury of the International Exhibition of 1862, specially noted the great improvement in dye, finish, and taste, shown in worsted goods; and the progress which has been made since that year may fairly bear comparison with the decade that preceded it. The manufacturers of the West Riding must still yield the palm to their French competitors in cloths composed entirely of wool, and manufactured for the richer classes of consumers; but Yorkshire stands unquestionably first in the production of the far larger group of fabrics intended for the middle and poorer ranks. These are the compound goods, in which the weft is worsted, alpaca, mohair, rheea, or some similar fibre, and the warp, cotton or silk. Of late years the West Riding has had to contend against growing and intelligent competition in foreign towns. Prussia and Belgium both endeavour to attract its peculiar class of customers. In France, up to the outbreak of the war of 1870, the race was maintained with equal vigour and skill. Such was the progress made in that country, that competent observers believed in its ultimate equality with England, as a home for manufacturers and commerce. The machinery at Roubaix in 1867 was five-fold what it had been in 1862. In 1870 the exports from France, of worsted goods alone, exceeded in value £11,000,000, against £6,500,000 of woollen and worsted goods combined in 1865. Striking as are these figures, Yorkshire, looking upon its own, has no reason to dread the competition they imply. They are spurs to renewed effort, not grounds for discouragement.

As the manufacture developed, and invention became busy, great changes came over the trade. The original makers of Norwich "says, russells, and worsted," are doubtless the real progenitors of our modern manufacturing chiefs, but the difference between the work of the earlier and the later times is immense. The foreign weavers who came over under Henry VII. and Elizabeth, brought with them new fabrics and industrial ability. Bombazines (1575), shalloons, serges, tammies, and a host of other names, figure among the records of two and three hundred years ago. Mr. James gives a list, from a Northamptonshire manufacturer, published in 1739, of thirty-nine separate classes of articles made from combing wool, eleven of combing and carding wool mixed, and twelve of long wool and silk, mohair, and cotton mixed. The writer adds that, there are "diverse other sorts of different stuffs, both figured, clouded, spotted, plain, and striped, too tedious to name." The introduction of cotton warps about 1834, which made it possible to have a lighter and cheaper material than worsted alone could give, extended and varied the trade in a startling manner. Of course the innovation caused great terror to many, and predictions of coming ruin abounded. But a little time dissipated these illusions. It was found that the new combination not only gave increased fineness of texture, but that it reduced the cost of production. The union of silk warps with worsted wefts, which followed, still further aided the resources of the manufacturer, by enabling him to produce goods possessing a delicacy, softness, and elasticity before unknown. The rise of the alpaca and mohair industry continued and augmented the impetus. The extent and importance to which these latter have attained render a separate notice of them necessary.

Among the staple products of the worsted district, those of alpaca and mohair have of late years risen into considerable prominence, mainly through the action of a gentleman whose charities, no less than his manufacturing and commercial enterprise, have won for him the deserved honour of a baronetcy, Sir Titus Salt, baronet, of Saltaire. The wool of the alpaca (the native Peruvian sheep) is superior to English wool in length, in softness, and in pliability. The difference in length, however, is less of late that in former years, owing to the more frequent shearings of the fleece. For a long time it was very difficult to get the wool at all, the Peruvians being unwilling to sell it, and the inconvenience of getting it from the mountain regions to the sea-coast being very great; besides, people here were almost ignorant of its existence, and there was no demand to stimulate enterprise. It appears to have been first brought to England in 1807, when a further attempt was made to bring it into use; but it was not till after an interval of twenty-three years that Mr. Outram, of Greetland, near Halifax, about 1830, succeeded in producing "an article which sold at high prices for ladies' carriage shawls and cloakings;" more, it is said, because they were rare and curious, than because they were intrinsically worth the money. Messrs. Wood & Walker, and Messrs. Horsfall, of Bradford, about the same time experimented in its manufacture; but the pieces displayed none of the lustre with which modern alpacas have made everybody familiar, and the enterprise came to an end for want of encouragement. Sir Titus Salt was the first to spin the alpaca wool into an even thread, and by combining it with cotton and silk warps, to create a new staple industry. Little progress was made so long as the alpaca weft was woven with worsted warps. It had no lustre and no lightness, but was heavy and unattractive. With cotton warps improvement became visible at once, and when woven with silk warps it was found that almost any perfection of finish and beauty could be attained. The trade has now come to be amongst the most valuable in the district.

The vast establishment at Saltaire is probably unequalled in the world for extent and completeness, and it is still rapidly growing. The mills, warehouses, stables, dining-hall for workpeople, dyehouse, sudworks, and gashouse, cover 9½ acres; 775 dwelling-houses, and 45 alms-houses, are spread over 25½ acres, and contain a population of 4356 (5⅓ per house); and a public park of 14 acres, given by the munificent founder, brings up the total extent to 49 acres. The sick and funeral societies number 2590 members, and out of the whole population only nine persons were in the receipt of parish relief in March, 1870. Sir Titus Salt has also built and handed over to trustees a Congregational church, which cost £16,000; has given a site for a Wesleyan chapel, and assistance towards the building; and has just erected the Saltaire Literary Institute and Club, for the use of the inhabitants, at a cost of £20,000. This institution, in respect of the amplitude and excellence of the resources it offers for the study and recreation of receivers of weekly wages, is unrivalled in the kingdom.

The second great modern branch of the Yorkshire trade is that in mohair, or goats' wool. This is exclusively foreign, the wool being brought by preference from the flocks fed on the dry chalk hills around Angora, in Asia Minor, although the lowland goats contribute also to the somewhat limited supply. One particular quality of wool is said to be altogether refused to foreigners. This consists of the female goat's fleece when two years old, and the selected hair of other white goats; the latter kind not amounting to one per cent. of the whole produce. It is kept at home for the manufacture of delicate gloves, hosiery, and dress stuffs, and exported only when in a finished state. English stuffs have, however, so far improved of late that they compete with the Turks in their own market, and have practically extinguished the native trade. The Yorkshire manufacturers of mohair, who are principally in the Bradford district, make it up into many fabrics, using with it cotton and silk warps, and the stuffs so produced possess a singular beauty and brilliance. Besides the great firms of Sir Titus Salt, Sons & Co.; John Foster & Sons, of Queensbury; and Messrs. Mitchell Brothers, of Bradford, whose splendid works count in the first rank of the palaces of industry which abound in the West Riding—there are many manufacturers of this wool scattered about and near Bradford, while both Norwich and Scotland are competitors, but scarcely rivals, in the trade.

The development of the manufacture would never have reached its present position, had not other influences come into play beyond the mechanical improvements to which we have referred. Plain greys are useful, but colour enters largely into the influences which cause textile fabrics to be admired and bought. For a long time dyers experienced great difficulty in imparting variety of colour to worsted stuffs. So long as they had to deal with one class of material only—with wool, for example, an exclusively animal product, or with cotton, a purely vegetable growth—their task was comparatively simple. It assumed another aspect when they had to deal with a mixture of the two. Surface colours might be produced, but they were fleeting; and the desideratum was to unite the colour and the cloth as permanently as possible. There is no "fast" colour until the dye-stuffs "have passed into a state of insoluble compound with the fibres themselves." In this matter of worsted the perplexity was increased by the necessity of dealing with two substances in one fabric, the chemical affinities acting upon one of which had no influence upon the other. So insuperable was this obstacle believed to be, that for a time the cotton warp was dyed before it was woven, and it was only possible to match the worsted weft with it in a very limited number of colours. The mordant or base of preparation for dyeing most in use, till about thirty years ago, was copperas; but about 1839 or 1840 bi-chromate of potash was introduced. This is perhaps the finest mordant in existence for receiving vegetable colouring matter, and its adoption completely revolutionized the trade, not only because it largely increased the number of colours obtained, but because of the great rapidity of its action. Before the use of bi-chrome a black dyed piece took one day to prepare and another to dye; the whole process can now be accomplished in two hours. Such had been the progress attained by 1855, that a committee appointed by the Bradford Chamber of Commerce to report on the productions of English as compared with those of foreign manufacturers and dyers shown at the Paris Exhibition, stated their conviction that "in mixed fabrics, when the difficulties presented by the combination of animal and vegetable substances have to be overcome, there was nothing in the Exhibition equal to the colours and effects produced by the Bradford dyers." The introduction of aniline colours in 1859 and 1860, gave an enormous impetus to the art, both in variety and extent; as also did the later practice of stoving or bleaching with sulphur, and tinting, which latter is in reality painting the material rather than dyeing it. By this last-named process the most beautiful tints are obtained, but they are unfortunately very evanescent.

The improvement of the machinery for dyeing remains to be briefly noticed. Until about 1839, dyeing vessels were made of tin, lead, or iron, and were all heated by fire. These were superseded by stone vessels heated by steam. Next came steam or roll boiling instead of water boiling, which avoided the "listing" or unequal dyeing of the pieces, and so saved the constant necessity of redyeing which attended the earlier system, as well as its cost, which in a large establishment was very great. New drying machines followed.

The old practice had been to dry pieces in long drying houses, with hot air—a slow process, and one requiring continual attention. The new process passes them over hollow tin cylinders heated by steam, and accomplishes in three minutes the task which hot air performed less perfectly in more than as many hours. With similar results as to increased speed, effectiveness, and economy, the ancient practice of dyeing in open vessels by manual labour gave place to machine-dyeing. On the former plan the dyeing of forty pieces required the constant attendance of five or six men; on the new one, a hundred pieces are dyed by a single machine, and two men and two boys will attend to three of them.

Until cotton warps began to be used with worsted weft, all dyeing establishments were small. Large works, like those of the present time, were altogether unknown. The founders of now leading houses dealt with single pieces where now they deal with hundreds, and in more than one notable instance the acting "market-man" was the dyer's wife, who went to Bradford or Halifax market with half a dozen warps or pieces, while her husband was attending to business at home. Not a generation ago, dyers still washed their fabrics in Ovenden brook or Bradford beck, but he would be a sanguine man who should hope to do anything but dye them, were he to immerse them now in those opaque rivulets of liquid soaps and chemicals.

There has long been one clearly marked distinction between the productions of the Yorkshire worsted district, and those of foreign countries. The Yorkshire manufacturers aim rather at extent of trade than expensiveness in the material they produce. Except in the alpaca and mohair industries, to which this statement is not equally applicable, the object sought is universality through cheapness. This distinction is not now so clear as formerly. Foreign rivals, in Prussia and Belgium principally, have of late years turned their attention in the same direction, and not without success; but still the broad difference remains that the special superiority of Yorkshire goods is in the cheaper varieties, and that of foreign goods in those which are more expensive.

The district in Yorkshire within which the worsted manufacture may be considered the staple industry, extends from Bradford, its metropolis, by Halifax westward to the border of Lancashire, and from Leeds by Shipley, Saltaire, Bingley, and Keighley, up the valley of the Aire to Cononley, near Skipton. Colne, just within the Lancashire border, also makes stuff pieces, and its manufacturers attend the Bradford Exchange. Wakefield, once an important worsted town, has now altogether ceased to be so. So completely is the trade now concentrated in Yorkshire, that (according to a Parliamentary return, dated 22nd July, 1868) out of 2,149,024 worsted spinning spindles in England, Yorkshire alone was then running 2,007,257, or more than nineteen-twentieths of the whole; out of 71,556 power-looms employed in England, there were 69,211 in Yorkshire; and out of 128,418 persons working in factories throughout the country, Yorkshire alone gave employment to 121,117. Almost the whole of the trade, it must be understood, is now carried on in factories. Here and there, in secluded dales branching out of the main valleys of the Aire and Calder, or on the lofty hill ranges which divide them, may be heard the weary click indicative of the hand-loom weaver's monotonous and ill-paid toil. But the application of steam to the manufacture made the extinction of domestic labour only a question of time. The yarn-spinners of the villages had no chance against the precise and rapid machinery of the towns, and the manufacturer was only too glad to save the time which he could much more profitably use in superintending his "works," than in traversing the Yorkshire hills and dales to distribute his material, and collect it when wrought up. The increased speed with which everything connected with the trade is transacted, is startling to men who remember the old times and ways. Time was, as men yet active in business well remember, when the Manchester merchant coming to Bradford market took three days for the outward and return journey. Starting from the cotton metropolis on Wednesday morning with a postchaise and pair of horses, one ridden by a postilion, he got as far as Halifax, where he stayed the night. Next day, by way of the lofty table-land of Catherine Slack and Queensbury (then Queenshead, and now the seat of one of the largest mohair manufactories in the kingdom) he reached Bradford, completed his business, dined, and returned to Halifax. On Friday, after his early breakfast, he saw his Halifax dyers or other business connections for an hour, and then away by

Todmorden and Blackstone Edge to Manchester again. The travellers by the Bradford and Manchester market express-train would think chaos come again were they to return, if only for a month, to the habits of their immediate predecessors.

Mr. John Milner, of Clayton, informs the writer that within his memory, dating from the beginning of the present century, the hand-shuttle was still used. There was no mechanical appliance to aid the weaver in propelling his shuttle across the warp. This had to be done with the fingers, and it was so done until the hand of a weaver was recognizable in the "hoofs" or callosities produced by the practice. At this time only hand-spun yarn was used, so coarse, in most cases, that it was exceedingly difficult to work it. The more prominent hairs, as they were called, were burnt off by the weaver, with an apparatus of candles fixed in a wooden framework, to the great danger of the warp and the probable loss of the work-man. The pieces then woven were calimancoes about nineteen inches wide, and nine candles were used in the operation. This plan became unnecessary after the invention of the "false reed," an arrangement of vertical wires, which cleared and smoothed the yarn in readiness for the shuttle. Then came the introduction into the district of the "picking-stick" or "fly-shuttle," about 1801. This rendered the work easier, but at its best it was monotonous, weari-some, and ill-paid. How miserable the scale of payment was is clear from the fact that, about 1800, a weaver at Clayton Heights offered, in a public house full of company, to make a bet that he alone, of all present, had woven a five shilling piece every week for twelve months. Now and then a man would have two to deliver in one week, but to do this would require him to work far into each night, and at least one night through. Then too, a shirt (four yards of Knaresborough cloth, says my informant) cost sixteen shillings, and few working people possessed more than one, going without or waiting in bed while it received its occasional cleansing. Nor were people more fortunate in the matter of provisions: flour, as an article of ordinary use, was unknown; oat-meal porridge and old milk formed the staple of food for the multitude. The first distinct change for the better in wages appears to have been made about 1805 or 1806, when manufacturers from Lancashire began to employ the weavers of Halifax, Bradford, and the adjacent villages in the fabrication of dimity and jeannettes at nine shillings per piece. This price, it must be remembered, included the dressing of the warp, which was then done by the weaver himself with brush and paste, and finished, tailor-fashion, by being ironed with a heated "goose."

Prior to the passing of the Factory Act in 1833, the children employed in the mills appear to have suffered exceedingly from habitual ill-usage and overwork. That Act provided that, during nine fixed hours of the night, there should be no work at all in factories; that no person under eighteen should labour more than sixty-nine hours a week; that no child under thirteen should work more than forty-eight hours; and that all children so employed should attend school for two hours on each working day in the week. Successive Acts have still further restricted the hours within which children and women are permitted to work in factories, and there can be no doubt as to the beneficial operation of the law. It is pleasant to note that a still further amelioration is in progress by mutual agreement between employers and their workpeople. The Saturday half holiday, beginning about two o'clock in the afternoon, conceded many years ago in most mills and warehouses throughout the district, is now in many instances begun at one o'clock, and in some as early as twelve. The fact of friendly agreement on such a subject is a striking proof of the growth of happier relations between the two classes than those which formerly prevailed, and may be set against the tendency to strikes which many people, not without reasonable grounds, look upon as one of the most threatening obstacles in the way of our future prosperity.

The social condition of the mass of the inhabitants in any of our crowded towns must always be more or less unsatisfactory. The essentials of healthy existence, light and air, are obscured and polluted by smoke, and the poisonous gases which the refuse of every great centre of population so easily generates. It is obvious that Bradford and Halifax cannot expect to have the freedom from disease, and certain other forms of evil, which falls to the lot of the dwellers in a country village. They must accept and make the best they can of the conditions of trade, overruling them wherever it is possible, and so contriving that only necessary dangers and dis-advantages may remain. It cannot be doubted that the current of events sets steadily in this direction now. The local authorities—

municipal at Bradford and Halifax, boards of health and so forth elsewhere—are actively prosecuting a praiseworthy crusade against dirt, foul air, tortuous streets, and gloomy courts and passages, at a cost against which many of the constituents vehemently protest. But there is no help for it. The rapid growth of these seething centres of industry has made it absolutely imperative that the blunders and ignorance of past generations should be remedied. As matters stand, the death rate is far higher than the average throughout England, and there is no reason to believe that this is so because of any exceptional character attaching to the worsted manufacture. There was a time, not half a century ago, when diseases brought on by the factory system, and peculiar to it, were sadly frequent; but Mr. Robert Baker (an excellent authority), writing in 1859, says, speaking of factories throughout the United Kingdom, "There is a gross increase of workers of 92 per cent., the increase of females being 131 per cent., and nearly as many children as there were formerly; and yet all the diseases which were specific to factory labour in 1832 have as nearly as possible disappeared." Eleven years have passed since Mr. Baker wrote, and the improvement which he noted then is not the less visible now.

As in all large towns, both in and out of Yorkshire, there is in the worsted district considerable waste and suffering caused by the intemperate use of beer and spirits. Drinking is made easy by the multiplication of facilities for its debasing enjoyments, and great numbers are too weak to resist the temptations which obtrude themselves at the corner of every street. Yet the case, though sad and disheartening, is not hopeless. The taint, if general, is far from universal, and dark as the prospect seems at present, we may surely hope that, as education becomes more general, as knowledge grows, and when the increased power of self-restraint which mental culture must create has had time to shape more wisely the lives of the people, that healthy and innocent recreations will take the place of excitements, which, beginning in physical indulgence, too often deaden every noble purpose, and give a fatal facility to crime.

One very satisfactory evidence of the prosperous condition of the inhabitants of the worsted district is found in the statistics of its financial institutions, such as building societies, savings banks, friendly and benefit societies, &c. Take, for example, the receipts of a few building and investment societies, the real object of which, it should be borne in mind, is not to purchase or build property as an organization, but to collect into a general fund the savings of persons who are willing to lend them, and to advance the sum so got together, on security of real property only, to another set of persons who desire to borrow. The Bingley Society shows in its last report (for 1869) a total receipt of £30,058; the Keighley and Craven Society (1870), £29,300; the West Riding Society (Halifax, 1870), £18,000; the Halifax Permanent (1869), £135,000; the Bradford Second Equitable (1870), £180,000; and the Bradford Third Equitable (1871), £430,000: making a grand total of £793,000.

There is considerable difficulty in arriving at a satisfactory estimate of the present value and extent of the worsted trade. Mr. Forbes, writing in 1851, gives the following tables as the result of his careful and elaborate calculations:—

WORSTED TRADE.—MR. FORBES' ESTIMATE, 1851.

60,000,000 lbs. English sorted wool at 1s. 2d. per pound, ...	£3,500,000
15,000,000 lbs. colonial and foreign, at 1s. 9d., "	1,312,500
Add other raw materials used in the manufacture, as cotton, silks, dyewares, &c., ...	1,500,000
Direct wages paid, ...	3,000,000
Indirect wages, as rent, wear and tear of machinery, coals, soap, oil, interest of capital &c., ...	3,187,500
Total, ...	12,500,000

DISTRIBUTED THUS :—

West Riding of Yorkshire, goods and yarns, ...	£8,000,000
Lancashire, delaines and other light fabrics, ...	1,500,000
Leicestershire, worsted hosiery, ...	1,200,000
Norwich goods, Irish stuffs, Devonshire long ells, &c., ...	1,300,000
Scotland, worsted stuffs (not including shawls), ...	500,000
Total, ...	12,500,000

Six years later Mr. John James, for his "History of the Worsted Trade," brought down the figures to 1857.

WORSTED TRADE.—MR. JAMES' ESTIMATE, 1857.

85,000,000 lbs. of English combing wool, sorted and washed, at 1s. 9d. per lb.,	£7,438,500
15,000,000 lbs. of colonial and foreign combing wool, sorted and washed, at 2s. 8d. per lb.,	2,000,000
Cotton warps used in the manufacture, silk warps and weft, dyewares, soap, oil, &c.,	1,700,000
Wages paid to 86,690 persons employed in factories,	1,861,500
Wages of sorters, combers, hand-loom weavers, dyers, &c.,	1,200,000
Rent of mills, wear and tear of machinery, warehouse rent, &c., interest of capital, and profits,	3,800,000
Total,	18,000,000

DISTRIBUTED THUS :—

West Riding of Yorkshire, goods,	£10,600,000
" " yarn for export, and sent to Glasgow, Norwich, Manchester, &c.,	3,100,000
Lancashire, coburgs, mousselines de laine, &c.,	2,000,000
Norwich goods, Devonshire long ells, carpets, &c.,	1,500,000
Leicestershire, worsted hosiery,	800,000
Total,	18,000,000

When the River Commissioners sat at Bradford in 1866, Mr. Jacob Behrens, afterwards president of the Bradford Chamber of Commerce, presented for their consideration a valuable series of estimates. He computed the value, in 1864, of the home and export trade in worsteds at £33,600,000, and the weight of wool used at 149,700,000 lbs.—an enormous advance upon previous calculations ; but the subject is one upon which Mr. Behrens is well qualified to speak with authority. The number of persons employed, given by Mr. James in 1857 as 86,690, had risen in 1867 to 128,410, an augmentation of one-half in ten years, and one which amply justifies the estimate of Mr. Behrens, when we consider the improved processes of late years, and the greatly-increased result of each individual person's labour.

WORSTED TRADE.—MR. BEHRENS' ESTIMATE.

£	EXPORTS	Lbs.
5,417,377	yarns (31,824,296 lbs.), equal in wool to	35,000,000
7,945,633	goods, ¼th mixed with other material, £6,000,000 wool (4s.), ...	30,000,000
2,852,815	do. all wool (4s.), ...	14,000,000

HOME.

13,200,000	goods, mostly mixed with other material (4s.), . . .	66,000,000
1,200,000	do. of mohair (5s.), ...	4,700,000
2,984,175	cotton and other material, worked up with the above, exclusive of exports, ...	
33,600,000		149,700,000

The following tables, which summarize the more important particulars affecting the trade, such as extent, wages, and population, may fitly conclude this sketch. The price of labour, as will be seen in the columns showing the rates of wages, is comparatively high ; indeed, taken all round, it has at no period been higher. The materials used are costly, and yet the trade grows and the exports annually increase. It is not so much by high profits on individual articles, as by the gains, singly small but vast in total, which are incident to enormous production, that the worsted district makes its gigantic returns.

The following table of the rate of wages in Bradford, Halifax, and the vicinity, is taken from the parliamentary return of Miscellaneous Statistics of the United Kingdom, part vii. 1869, and may be regarded as authoritative : —

WORSTED MANUFACTURE—RATE OF WAGES.
HALIFAX AND NEIGHBOURHOOD.

Description of Occupation.		Rate of Wages per Week.	Hours of Labour.
Wool sorters, ...	{ Men, ...	18s. 6d. to 28s.	54 to 57½
	{ Boys, ...	12s.	60
Wool washers, . . .	Men, ...	12s. to 22s.	"
Wool carders, ...	Women, ...	9s. to 9s. 6d.	"
Machine wool combers,	{ Men, ...	12s. to 15s.	"
	{ Women, ...	9s. to 9s. 6d.	"
Makers up, ...	{ Boys, ...	10s.	"
	{ Women, ...	9s. to 10s.	"
Dyers, ...	Men, ...	14s.	"
Drawers, ...	Women and girls, .	8s. to 10s.	"
Spinners, ...	(Women,*	6s. 6d. to 8s.	"
	{ Boys,†	1s. 3d. to 4s.	30
	(Girls,†	1s. 3d. to 4s.	"
Twisters, ...	Girls, ...	8s. to 10s.	60
Reelers, ...	Women and girls, .	9s. to 14s.	"
Oilers, ...	Boys, ...	9s.	"
Jobbers, ...	Boys, ...	8s. to 10s.	"
Bobbin setters, ...	Boys, ...	5s.	"
Doffers, ...	Boys, ...	6s. 3d.	"
Weavers (piece work), .	(Men, ...	14s. to 20s.	"
	{ Women, ...	13s. to 18s.	"
	(Girls, ...	14s.	"
Overlookers, ...		18s. to 25s.	"
Assistant do.		13s. 6d. to 16s.	"
Engine tenters, . . .	Men, ...	22s. to 30s.	60 to 72
Engine feeders, ...		15s. to 18s.	60
Engine stokers, ...		14s. to 18s.	60 to 72
Mechanics, smiths, and joiners, ...	{ Men, ... { Boys, ...	20s. to 30s. 8s.	60 "
Packers, ... Warehousemen, . . .	} Men, ...	{ 15s. to 25s. { 15s. to 30s.	" "

Hours of labour generally—Mill, 60 hours per week.
Warehouse, 57 hours per week.

* Full timers.   † Short timers.

BRADFORD AND NEIGHBOURHOOD.

Description of Occupation.		Rate of Wages per Week.	Hours of Labour.
Wool sorters, ... {	Men, ...	28s.	60
	Boys, ...	12s.	"
Wool washers, . . .	Men, ...	17s. 6d.	"
Dyers, ... {	Men, ...	20s.	"
	Boys, ...	8s. to 12s.	"
Machine wool combers, {	Men, ...	15s.	"
	Boys, ...	8s. 6d.	"
	Women, ...	9s. 6d.	"
Drawers, ...	Women, ...	10s. to 12s.	"
Reelers, ...		10s.	"
Weavers, ...		12s.	"
Overlookers, ...	Men, ...	30s.	"
Assistant do.		10s. to 28s.	"
Engine tenters, . . .		28s. to 35s.	"
Engine feeders, ...		20s.	"
Engine stokers, ...		20s.	"
Mechanics, smiths, and	Men, ...	28s.	"
joiners, ...	Boys, ...	6s. to 11s.	"
Heads of Department—			
In dyehouses, ...		30s. to 50s.	—
Finishers and warehousemen, ...		Vary very much according to circumstances.	—

TABLE SHOWING THE PROGRESS OF THE WORSTED MANUFACTURE IN
ENGLAND AND THE WEST RIDING SINCE 1838. EXTRACTED FROM THE
PARLIAMENTARY RETURNS.

ENGLAND.

	1838.	1850.	1856.	1861.	1868.
Factories, ...	415	493	511	512	687
Horse-power, ...	7,166	11,270	14,483	27,093	45,140
Spindles, ...		864,874	1,298,326	1,245,526	2,149,024*
Power-looms, ...		32,617	38,809	42,968	71,556
Persons employed, ...	31,606	78,915	86,690	82,972	128,410

* And 335,039 doubling spindles.

WEST RIDING.

	1838.	1850.	1861.	1861.	1868.	Yorkshire. Horse-powe 1868.
Factories, . . .	348	418	445	443	626	17,614
Horse-power, . .	5,791	9,389	12,723		42,494	563
Spindles, ...		746,281	1,212,587	1,149,072	2,007,257	3,889
Power-looms, . .		30,856	35,298	40,577	69,211	148
Persons employed,	29,336	70,905	78,994	76,483	121,117	19,255
						880
						141
						4
						42,494

GLOSSARY

ALPACA

The auchenia paco of zoology, generally known as a species of the lama domesticated in Peru, possessing a long silky fleece. The fine lustrous cloth woven with yarn spun from alpaca wool, also used to describe worsted or union cloths imitating alpaca.

The use of alpaca really became important in Yorkshire following the work of Sir Titus Salt; he found a satisfactory way of processing it, and the industry in alpaca and also in mohair which followed was important, not only for the fame of the firm of Salt's of Saltaire but for the whole worsted trade of Yorkshire.

BAIZE

Baize, like duffel, was and is a fairly cheap cloth, but it is always relatively light in weight, not more than 16 oz per yd, 56 in wide, usually raised but not given the complicated dress finish of the super-fine broadcloth. The word derives from bays, presumably used normally in the plural and so became baize. It occurs as early as 1578 and was probably one of the New Draperies. Now normally green, but it is not certain whether this has always been the case.

BAR

Or bar-tree, sometimes plural, the frame upon which the warp is wound in hand warping.

BICHROMATE OF POTASH (CHROME)

Baines correctly stresses the importance of the change to, or rather the development of, chrome as a mordant. Few writers have realised, or at least stressed, this sufficiently. Today it is the almost universally used mordant for wool; indeed the group of fast dyes that need a mordant are simply called chrome dyes. In the past, different mordants were used to get different colours from the same natural dyes.

Baines' reference to black is interesting. Before the introduction of a chrome mordant it was difficult to obtain a good black, but logwood on chrome gave one and was universally used until the introduction of the aniline blacks around 1900, dyes, incidentally, which

145

K

also need a chrome mordant.

Logwood when first put to use in the sixteenth century was dyed on other mordants mainly to give a cheaper blue than was obtained from indigo, and its poor fastness gave it a bad name, eg the devil's dye. When used as a black on a chrome mordant this drawback did not occur.

BRITCH

Sometimes breech. The wool grown on the hindquarters of the sheep near the tail. An interesting word, traditional in the English wool trade but not widely used elsewhere. What we know as Britch is elsewhere locks, stained pieces, brands, bellies, etc.

The word is no longer used in British wool-marketing sales, being usually replaced by dags, a word which is certainly also old: the *Oxford English Dictionary* gives a definition dated 1731, 'one of the locks of wool clotted with dirt from the hind quarters of the sheep'.

BROADCLOTH

Originally simply meant cloth woven on a broad-loom, that is anything from 56 in to 72 in wide when finished, but it later came to be applied more specifically to the type of cloth made by first fulling and then clothworking. As Baines says, 'Super-fine broadcloth was the hall-mark of quality in the woollen textile trade'. At the time he was writing, broadcloths were manufactured of the finest merino wool, which during the eighteenth century came from Spain, then for a short period from Germany. The Australian wool that was to replace all the others was beginning to come regularly to Britain at the time that Baines was first writing.

When woven on a broad handloom, woollen broadcloth was made in the plain weave, that is every alternative end and pick worked exactly opposite to its neighbours; there were only two different kinds of interlacings and consequently only two harnesses were needed. Later versions, that is power-loom woven, such as doeskins, used more complicated patterning.

BURLING

The word has an interesting textile history. Today to 'burl' means to pick out foreign matter, including vegetable impurities such as burr. But there is no connection between the two words burl and burr. Sometimes vegetable impurities can be covered by a dye that colours vegetable but not animal substance, and this process is called burl-dyeing. There has obviously been a semantic confusion. The emphasis on vegetable impurity has only come with the wide use of Australian wool; native English wool, and as far as our information goes the Spanish merino wool, was much less contaminated.

It would be interesting to know whether the word in any way derives from the burel, a cloth widely made in medieval times but then disappearing. London, Winchester and Marlborough all made burels. They were coarse cloths, as Chaucer's lines clearly indicate :

> But Sires because I am a Burel Man
> At my beginning first I you beseech
> Have me excused from my rude speech.
>
> (*The Franklin Prologue*, lines 44-47)

BURRS

The spiny seeds of the burdock or prickly heads of grasses and plants which attach themselves to wool. The word became more and more common with the wide use of Australian wool. Burrs can be removed by treating with an acid (carbonising) or passing through special machines (peraltas).

CALIMANCOES

A difficult word. I suspect a derivation from calico, possibly calico-madams. See Lipson, *Economic History*, vol 3, p 43, 'the use of printed Calicos prohibited. Appeals were made to women to discard the new fashion and the weavers raised a great clamour, created disturbances and attacked in the open streets the wearers of cotton stuffs, the Calico-madams or Calico-ruts as they were called'.

Norwich then set about manufacturing fancy worsteds to copy these calico prints, and for a typical example of misplaced industry see the pattern book of their efforts in the Public Record Office. According to Heaton (p 270), calimancoes were being made in Yorkshire by 1750. Arthur Young in 1770 noted that they were being

147

made in Leeds, 'the heart of the woollen trade'. 'Some Shalloons and many other stuffs, particularly Scotch Camlets, Grogans and Calimancoes, etc'.

CAMLETS

There are several alternatives for this word—camblets, camblettes, camelots. All were fabrics woven of cotton and wool having a waved surface. According to the *Oxford English Dictionary*, 'the word originally was used for a costly Eastern fabric, then for the substitutes indicated'. Shakespeare has an interesting use: 'stuffs made from the hair of the Angora goat, known among us by the name of Camlet'; but this never appears to have been generally accepted.

The *Oxford English Dictionary* derives the word from the French Camelot, which is associated with the word camel, and probably comes itself from the Arabian klamlet—pile or nap.

The *Shakespearian Glossary* notes: 'A fabric which has varied considerably in material; in the sixteenth and seventeenth century made of the hair of the Angora goat', and gives as reference *Henry VIII*, act 5, scene 4, line 95.

Heaton, p 274, comments: 'Even Leeds, stalwart heart of the woollen body, was partly captured by worsted stuffs'. And Arthur Young, when there, noted that in addition to broadcloths many other cloths were made. The camlet was the chief, and consisted of rough worsted material, considered especially valuable for resisting rain and therefore used to a great extent in the making of cloaks and wraps for those who were travelling by coach. It also formed the customary dress material of the poorer class of women. The substitution of lighter cloths, the adoption of the mackintosh and the growth of the railroad rendered these camlets unfashionable, and Leeds returned to its first love, the woollen.

COBURG

Was a fine cloth originally composed of silk warp and merino weft, but made popular by using cotton for the silk. The word appears to have been first used in 1882 and comes from the German province—obviously there is a link with Prince Albert.

148

CONDENSERS

Even after scribbling, carding and spinning had been mechanised, there remained an unfortunate break in the sequence of woollen-yarn manufacture. The opened raw material was knocked off the back end of the last carding roller by the doffing comb, invented by Arkwright or Hargreaves, and rolled into lengths of sliver the width of the carding machine. These pieces of sliver had to be laboriously pieced together before being given a modicum of twist on the billy.

Various rather clumsy attempts were made in Britain to do away with this hand process, and there were several versions of so-called piecing machines. All these ignored the fact that a satisfactory alternative system, called condensing, had already been worked out in America. The germ of this idea came from various sources, but the production of a successful method was the work of John Goulding of Massachusetts. He used a ring doffer (the doffer is the name given the last roller on the card), and instead of having the strips of card wire running across the card, placed them around it and consequently produced endless ribbons of sliver, which were rubbed into a round sliver by pairs of leather rollers.

Later the ring-doffer method of dividing the carding material was replaced by a tape condenser, where first metal and later rubber dividers performed the same work. Today the leather tape condenser is almost universal.

COTTON WARP

Baines' emphasis on cotton warps in the worsted trade is important and sometimes forgotten, because in the second half of the nineteenth century these cotton warps almost entirely disappeared from the scene, and the typical worsted cloth made then and during the first half of the twentieth century was 100 per cent wool. After 1950 the position changed again and many so-called worsted cloths now contain a proportion of synthetic fibre, usually intimately mixed with the wool and not as a separate warp.

The use of the cotton warps enabled power-looms to be used for worsted fabrics long before they were really satisfactory for woollens.

It should be remembered that when Baines was writing the combing process had only just been mechanised and had not reached the degree of perfection enabling it to produce strong, fine yarns; nor, incidentally, were the outstanding combing merino wools yet available in large quantities from Australia.

CROSS BAND (OPEN BAND)

Twisting yarn can be done in two ways, today indicated by S; Z. In the past these twists were often called cross or open band, the point being that the strings driving each individual spindle in the mule could be either cross or open, giving the two alternative twists.

In order to obtain heavily milled cloths it was common to use one twist for warp and another for weft. This is not so common today as it does lead to problems of stock-holding, etc.

The direction of the twist is important in designing and, as one type of twist is normally used in the warp, with herring-bones the twill to the right shows more distinctly than that to the left.

DAMASKS

Were a rich, silk stuff, woven of coloured warp and weft figured all over, usually twilled. The word was also used to describe a kind of Scotch carpet, the pattern being worked in with the warp rather than the weft. The *Oxford English Dictionary* goes further back and gives damask as usually produced at Damascus, either as (1) a rich silk fabric woven with elaborate figures (also applied to fabrics of wool, linen or cotton); or (2) a twilled linen fabric with designs which are shown up by the opposite reflections of light on the surface, and used chiefly for table linen.

The different light reflections are caused by the weave changing, usually warp-to weft-faced on a satin-weave basis.

DELAINE

In other words of 'wool'. Fabricwise a class of wool muslin, but now mostly woven with mixed yarns. The *Oxford English Dictionary* defines it as a light textile fabric for women's dresses, originally of wool, now usually of wool and cotton. The word is rarely met with today, but the afgalaine is the same thing, being a light wool or worsted dressweight fabric made in a crepe weave.

A somewhat similar word, mousselin de laine, was a fine cloth of open texture, woven with yarn composed of wool and cotton, in other words rather like Viyella. The word derives from the French *mousselin*=muslin, clearly an interesting reference to the French capacity to spin wool fine.

DEWING

Lawson's point about putting the pieces out in the open to take up the dew is interesting. Obviously conditioning was sought. Wool and its moisture content is an interesting subject, but this method of obtaining the necessary water is rarely met. It must however have been relatively common and is likely to explain the use of the name 'dewing machine'.

DIMITY

A cotton cloth woven with reversing twills so as to present a crimpled or ridged surface. The *Oxford English Dictionary* definition of a stout cotton cloth woven with raised stripes and fancy figures, used undyed for beds and hangings, and sometimes for garments, is rather narrow.

DOBBIES

When used for cloth the description derives from the loom name. A normal loom definition is of a machine used for operating healds shafts in looms capable of controlling twenty-four healds shafts and governed by pegged bars called lags in their motion.

The dobby loom lies partway between the plain two-harness loom as used for making the broadcloth, and the draw-loom, and the later jacquard, of almost unlimited possibilities. The dobby loom became the most widely-used loom in the West Riding woollen and worsted industries during the second half of the nineteenth century and has so continued.

DRAWERS

A word that has changed its meaning. In Baines, and generally in all documents describing the cloth trade at the time, it defines those people who put right faults that occur in weaving—broken ends, etc. Today we describe these workers as menders, and a drawer is the person who pulls or draws the individual warp ends through the heddles in the harness, a job that was originally considered to be one of the hand-loom weaver's duties.

DRESSING

Or perhaps, better, cloth-working: the traditional finish given to woollen cloth. The surface of the fabric was raised by being rubbed with teasels, in Baines's time, still often inserted in hand frames, but since placed in circular revolving rollers. Teasels have long been used for this purpose; with their hooked ends, they should be distinguished from the straight-end teasel which, before the introduction of wire cards, had been used for opening or teasing the wool before spinning. The word card, or carding, derives from the Latin name for teasels.

After raising the surface of the cloth, the nap—as it was usually called—was cut down by the hand shears and later the cutting machine. Frequently this series of operations was repeated several times, giving a skin-like appearance to the cloth. The best effect was obtained by carrying out these closely allied processes of raising and cutting when the cloth was wet. Today, few woollen cloths are given this treatment. Perhaps the best illustration of what was obtained is seen with the billiard cloth, but at one time all the best woollens (but not worsted) cloths were given this finish and were known by a variety of names, doeskin, buckskins, venetians, etc. As all billiard players know, these cloths have a definite 'way' on them, and this makes the manufacture of the garment more difficult.

DUFFEL

Has always meant a fairly heavy, comparatively cheap, woollen cloth, the type of fabric that Yorkshire has always made better than anyone else. The type of fabric used for the duffel coat today can be taken as typical. The word derives from the town of that name near Antwerp.

EAST INDIAN WOOL

Is the coarsest of all and almost entirely used for carpet manufacture. For carpets a different type and quality of wool is required, one with great resilience, and this the coarse East Indian wool possesses in abundance. These wools are also mixed in quality, containing relatively fine fibres mixed with coarse, a property desirable with carpets but to be deplored elsewhere.

With woven or knitted fabrics the strength of the fabric depends on the strength of the yarn, which admittedly depends somewhat on the length and strength of the wool, but also on the size of the yarn. But with the usual type of carpet—pile carpets—the crucial quality required in the fibre is the capacity to spring back— resilience—after being walked upon.

EVERLASTING

According to the Oxford English Dictionary 'that will never wear out' (1590), which does not help much. Probably there is an identification, as far as cloth is concerned, with Perpetuanas—met as an alternative name to serges in the Exeter trade. The chief reason for the supremacy of serges was that they satisfied a large demand for a wool fabric intermediate between the heavy and expensive broadcloth and the light Norwich stuffs.

FELTING

Under the microscope the surface of wool appears like a serrated edge, due to the presence of overlapping cells. It was usual in Baines's time to regard felting as due to the fibres interlocking. This is not strictly true; indeed, if the fibres did actually interlock there would be no movement and therefore no felting.

The important point is that as these cells with their protruding edges point all one way from root to tip, they encourage movement in one direction, when under the influence of warmth and moisture, but virtually prevent it in the other. Consequently once the fibres have been rubbed into a felted mass they will not disentangle. If all the surface serrations are removed, then felting will not take place —there is free movement in both directions; removal of the surface serrations is the most common way of preventing felting and therefore the capacity of the wool garment to shrink.

Incidentally, it is not true that the process of worsted spinning destroys the felting power of wool. The straight-fibre structure of the worsted yarn makes it a little less liable to felt than the crisscross arrangement in the woollen. But a worsted cloth will felt if it is subjected to warmth, moisture and pressure—in other words, if it is fulled.

Worsted fabrics are not normally fulled because they do not need felting to gain extra strength, and usually a clear-cut un-fulled appearance is being sought.

FETTLER

Baines's use of the word is one of the earliest there is. Fettlers clean the carding machines. As the wool passes through the scribblers and carders the dirt (vegetable impurities etc) in the wool is to a large extent left in the card wire. After a time it has to be removed, or the carding becomes inefficient. This cleaning is done with hand frames which closely resemble the original hand cards. Fettling, a hard and dirty occupation, remains today an important section of the work in the carding department.

GEARS

The alternative name for healds or heddle.

The healds are cords with rings or loops through which the warp ends are threaded for shedding purposes. They may be either of cord or wire; hence also heald-shafts, the horizontal lathes on which the healds are knitted if of cord, or slipped upon if of wire. The shafts are connected with the shedding appliance for lifting or depressing the warp thread passed through the eyes.

A number of words derive from heald and heddle, eg heddling, now usually called drawing.

GOOSE

Has meant many things, but the only textile-manufacturing one occurs in garment-making, where a goose is a tailor's smoothing-iron (plural gooses, not geese) of which the handle resembled a goose's neck. Shakespeare knew this use of the word: in Macbeth II, scene 3, line 17 we read 'come in Tailor, here you may roast your goose' (1605). The word was also used as a verb, to press or iron with a tailor's goose (1808).

HANDLE SETTER

The handles were the frames in to which the teasels were set.

It was a skilled job and the handles were kept in a warm moist atmosphere, usually in a special room where the bricks were left half open, that is brick and space; such buildings can still be seen in many mills.

HANK

A hank of yarn is a continuous length formed into a skein, the normal form in which knitting yarn is sold. It is also the length of yarn commonly accepted as a basis of measuring yarn size. Baines uses the word in this sense, stating that a cotton yarn had been spun to a fineness of 300 to 500 hanks in a pound—in other words what would now be called 300s to 500s, certainly very fine yarn.

He also states that 'worsted yarn seldom exceeds in fineness 100 hanks of 560 yards each', thereby establishing the fact that the new system of reckoning worsted yarn sizes in terms of the number of hanks that weigh 1 lb was already being used. 100s is very fine; most worsted yarns today are spun to between 32s and 48s. It would be interesting to know when this system of yarn measurement was first used. Incidentally, it became linked with wool fineness, and 64s wool means wool of such a fineness that a 64s worsted yarn represents the limit of its spinning capacity.

Woollen yarns are measured on a different basis, in Yorkshire the number of hanks of 256 yd that weigh 1 lb.

JEANNETTE

Presumably derived from jean, a word certainly well known today and the traditional textile description of a stout cotton twill woven with three healds, or a strong union cloth with a sateen face twill.

The word derives from Genoa and was originally a twilled cotton cloth, a kind of fustian. The description Genoa fustian was shortened to jean, and is first met with in 1488. 'Fustian' described a strong, twilled cotton cloth with a pile weft, a velveteen, corduroy or moleskin, thick-set; but probably, like so many words, it was often used in a wider sense.

The *Oxford English Dictionary* derives fustian from Fostat, a suburb of Cairo, where the stuff was first made, and describes it as 'normally a coarse cloth made of cotton and flax'. Now a thick twill cotton cloth with a short pile and nap, usually dyed a dark colour; also a blanket of this material. The word was widely used by Shakespeare: 'The serving men in their new Fustians'. Also generally, meaning bombastic.

JACQUARD LOOMS

The jacquard loom was invented by Jean Maire Jacquard of Lyons, and derived from the old draw loom known in the East from comparatively early times. On it fabrics with very complex interlacings and designs can be made.

The complexity of design depends on the different number of interlacings. The plain weave needs two different interlacings and is woven on a loom (the broadloom) with two harnesses; the common twill needs four harnesses, and during the days of handloom weaving was woven on a treadle loom arranged to work them. Such fabrics are now woven on a dobby loom, which can handle weaves of sixteen to twenty-four harnesses. But with Jacquard looms many more different interlacings are used—up to well over a thousand—and here, instead of harnesses, there are a number of headles, arranged in groups, controlled by a tie. These ties Jacquard controlled by stamped cards rather like a pianola, and indeed the jacquard can claim to be one of the earliest forms of automatic control.

KERSEYMERE

A corruption of cassimere, a name given to a fine twilled cloth first made in the West of England at Bradford-on-Avon, following an invention of a clothier there named Yerbury.

Cassimeres were finely spun and woven in the twill as opposed to the plain weave. Fitting in well with the demand for lighter cloths, they sold well and kept certain parts of the West of England, notably Trowbridge, busy until around 1825, when cassimeres themselves were replaced by worsteds.

Cassimeres were woven in narrow looms, not broadlooms as with the traditional broadcloth, and although made first in the Westcountry they were, as Baines's figures show, common in Yorkshire. Gott printed fancy patterns on them.

Kersey is quite different, a coarse cloth made in Yorkshire from the fourteenth century and sometimes called northern dozens. The name derives from an East Anglian cloth-making town of that name, an attractive village well worth visiting with a pleasant cloth church.

LISTS

The edge of the cloth. There are often complaints that weavers have used odd and poor yarn for their lists. It does not matter if odd yarn is used, but poor, that is tender, yarn should not be employed: the warp ends at the edge (the list or listing ends) have to bear more strain than any others, and continual breaking of the ends will greatly reduce weaving efficiency. Today we use the same yarn for this as for the rest of the cloth, and in the case of any difficulty extra-strong yarns.

An interesting derivation of the word list is lister, the alternative word for dyer: during dyeing, with certain weaves more than with others, the list tends to roll towards the centre of the cloth. The dyer therefore has continually to unroll the list—hence the name. It is a most unpleasant job as the dyeing is carried out in a boiling dye-bath.

LONG ELLS

An ell, of course, is the standard measurement of cloth lengths, which varied in different parts of the country: Scottish ells, 37.2 in; English, 45 in; Flemish, 27 in; French, 54 in.

I have not traced the origin of long ells; the actual cloths known as long ells were made in considerable quantities in the worsted trade centred around Exeter. They were made of coarse (local) wool, and sold in large quantities to the East India Company.

MERINO

Wool can, from the point of view of the cloth manufacturer, be divided into two sections: (1) the merino; (2) the rest. Or in other words, into fine wool produced by the merino sheep, animals grown primarily as wool-producers, and coarser wool from sheep whose meat production is more important than wool. Today all British breeds come in the second category.

The merino sheep originated in Spain, and from the fifteenth to the eighteenth century Spanish merino was the only fine wool available. For centuries strict laws prevented the export of any merino sheep from Spain, but gradually this strict law was allowed to lapse and the merino spread fairly widely, with German growers devoting great attention to breeding; indeed German merino wool was probably the finest ever grown, and was used between 1800 and 1850 for the superfine broadcloth.

Then the merino sheep was taken to Australia and that country quickly became the main area for fine-wool production, although useful quantities also came from South Africa, South America and, until the introduction of refrigeration, New Zealand.

MERINO (AS A CLOTH NAME)

This of course derives from the wool, specifically a twilled worsted cloth for dress goods. Also used as a yarn definition—yarn made from doubled worsted and cotton—which is misleading. The Oxford English Dictionary states 'a soft woollen material like French cassimere and second a fine woollen yarn used for hosiery', which in some ways is correct. Torn-up hosiery yarns are still called merinos, which is even more misleading.

Merino as a cloth definition was mainly a French term. The French were much better spinners of fine worsteds in the second half of the nineteenth century, partly because they still used mules. The problem of frame spinning of really fine wool took a considerable time in solving, particularly the finding of the correct type of roller covering.

MOREENS

A woollen cloth used for curtains and hangings, sometimes partly of cotton. The word first appears in 1691, and stress is sometimes laid on moreens having a watered effect—possessing a waving pattern on the surface of the fabric obtained by pressure and heat. The Oxford English Dictionary says: 'The word is perhaps derived from Moire, a form of silk Damask, pressed to give the surface a cloudy or wavy or watered appearance'; in other words a watered silk.

ORLEANS

The cotton grown in Mississippi and elsewhere from the gossypium hirsurtum, considered the most useful and regular of American cottons and consequently a cloth woven of cotton warp of this type crossed by wool weft. More generally a fabric of cotton warp and worsted weft brought alternatively to the surface in weaving.

PETERSHAM

A heavy woollen cloth, its hairy surface rolled into little knots. According to the *Oxford English Dictionary* the word was used in 1872 and derives from Viscount Petersham. It applied to heavy overcoats or breeches, and to the cloth from which such garments were then made.

PICKER

The small block of wood or leather which impels the shuttle across the web. The word was not used widely, if at all, before 1800 and in the sense we know it today comes from John Kay's invention of the flying shuttle.

PORTER

Twenty splits of a reed, or forty warp threads, is a normal textile definition, and presumably comes from the traditional manner of reeding or slaying the plain weave—that is two ends in a split.

The word must have come from 'portare'—to carry—and thus from the number of warp ends the warper carried in his hands as he was warping. It was also used as a method of counting the warp ends in the warp: thus forty portares would be 40 x 40=1600 ends. But was forty the recognised number? I have heard the West of England porter was only thirty-eight ends. The phrase is not now used, and there are no 'folk' records.

POTTING (OR ROLL-BOILING)

An interesting process developed in the West of England for superfine broadcloths. The cloth, after the raising and cutting had produced the dress finish, was rolled on to a roller and was placed for a long period (up to twenty-four hours) in a tank of boiling water. Owing to the complex chemical and physical structure of the wool fibre this gave a permanent set to the fabric. Incidentally the scientific basis of this process is identical to that used when giving human hair a permanent wave. Potting or roll-boiling provided one of the severest tests that dye stuff could be required to stand.

Today only billiard cloths and a few other specialised fabrics are potted, although most are given a kind of similar treatment by being rolled on a perforated roller with steam blown through.

In addition to fixing the finish, potting, and to a lesser extent the modern steam blowing, prevents any further shrinking.

PRUNELLES

Prunelle is the three-end twill-warp flush weave and obviously derives from the French. The *Oxford English Dictionary* does not give this word, but does give prunella (1656), derived from the French prunelle (origin obscure), and defines it as a strong 'stuff', originally silk, afterwards worsted, normally used for graduates', clergymen's and barristers' gowns, also later for the upper part of women's shoes.

Today the word is well known and is the name given to the two-and-one twill (three ends, as compared with common twill's four ends). This is usually made in the warp form (that is warp finish), but the term is equally applicable to the weft version which is usually called the weft prunelle. It is a fine twill and good for waterproofing in the warp form, but is not as adaptable for designing as the common (that is the two-and-two) twill.

QUARTER

A quarter of a yard, that is nine inches: this is the almost universal measurement for width. Thus normal-width cloth is 6 quarters =54 in. Narrow cloth, 3 quarters=27 in, is still occasionally made for riding tweeds and vestings. These two measurements of course derive from the broad and narrow loom.

RHEEA OR RHEE

Is the alternative name for the ramie, the popular name of the fibre obtained from the inner bark of the plant boehmeria nivea—china grass or nettle fibre, which is much less used than formerly, because of the introduction and consequent competition of man-made fibres; indeed it is probably not used in any form in the Yorkshire wool-textile trade today.

RUSSELLS

Russell cord was a worsted cloth of a fine cord twill, first made in Norwich. There was also a russel, a much older kind of woollen fabric (in use 1488), the term probably comes from the Flemish.

Much more common now of course is russet (derived from Russell?), described by the *Oxford English Dictionary* as a coarse home-spun woollen cloth of reddish-brown, grey or neutral colour, formerly used for the dress of peasants and country folk. Shakespeare knew the word well, and in *Love's Labours Lost*, act 5, scene 2, line 414, says : 'In Russet yea's and honest Kersey noes'. Certainly a significant and interesting word for all interested in textile history. Incidentally, what if anything was the difference between a russet and a kersey?

SCRIBBLING

The sequence of processes of converting wool into yarn is complicated, as Baines points out, and the scribbling perhaps calls for a more detailed description. The willeying and teasing only gave a very rough opening, and it was with the scribbling that the real removal of entanglements in wool began. At first hand cards were used, but by the time Baines was writing the wool was scribbled on a machine whose rollers were covered with card wires. The machine derived from the cotton card invented in a circular form by Daniel Bourn of Leominster and made a really practical mill machine by Richard Arkwright.

After scribbling, the wool is further opened and disentangled by being carded, the wire used on the hand card or the machine card being finer set (more points per square inch); as a result small entanglements are removed.

Some confusion has been caused by the fact that the whole process of removing these entanglements, the scribbling and the carding, and today also the condensing, are collectively known as carding.

161

L

SELVEDGE

An alternative name for list, sometimes selvage : the edges woven on to cloth to prevent fraying, and generally of a firmer texture than the body of the web. The *Oxford English Dictionary* gives an early use (1460) derived from self edge : 'The edge of a piece of woven material finished in such a manner as to prevent ravelling out of the weft. Also a narrow strip or list at the edge of a web of cloth which is intended to be cut off or covered by the seams when the material is made up'.

The description here should have been 'woven' in such a manner, not 'finished'.

SERGES

Worsted cloth woven in a broad twill, equal on both sides, in other words the two-and-two or common twill.

There are many other uses of the word : (1) fabric with the warp of worsted and the weft of woollen, sometimes of linen, mainly used for clothing; (2) a garment made of serge; (3) silk serge, a silk fabric twilled in the manner of serge, used for luxury coats and formerly for mantles.

Serges were one of the 'New Draperies' and the great product of the Exeter (Devon - Somerset) industry. These fabrics had a worsted warp and woollen weft, but over the centuries the word came to be used for worsted warp and worsted weft cloth, of which the navy-blue serge, so fashionable forty years ago, was a typical example.

SHALLOONS

One of the most common worsted materials, made originally in Norwich and then in Yorkshire; indeed, the rise in the worsted trade there in the eighteenth century rested largely on the successful making of shalloons.

Sam Hill was perhaps the leading exponent of this new trade, and his notebook is full of interesting information about the difficulties encountered : 'I am studying to out-do all England with the sort of Sam Hill Shalloons, if quality and price will do it, but must earnestly beg of you to let them go for a small profit however until they be known'.

The word derives from the French *chalon*, and according to the

Oxford English Dictionary, which incidentally mistakenly describes them as woven woollens, is first met in 1688; but probably Norwich was manufacturing this type of fabric earlier.

SHODDY AND MUNGO

Torn-up rags, which are then re-used to make a cheap cloth. Baines brings out the importance of this trade extremely well. It probably arose because of the relative scarcity and high price of new wool.

The famous and infamous nature of this material is clearly shown by the widespread use of the word to mean second-rate. It would perhaps be as well to indicate that the word was first used in its woollen sense. The *Oxford English Dictionary* gives 1832 but origins are obscure, and it only acquired its new and more common general meaning later—1862, according to the *Oxford English Dictionary*.

Shoddy was originally made by tearing up unmilled cloth; as the demand for this type of material grew, manufacturers began to tear milled materials, thereby obtaining a shorter raw material, called mungo; and the traditional origin of this word is that the carder complained that it would not go, that is spin, and the manufacturer said it 'mun go'.

The still lower waste is called fud, and is used for manure.

SIZING

The process by which the work was sized (ie given additional strength). The word 'size' means any viscous substance used for stiffening and bonding fibres or fabrics. The *Oxford English Dictionary* shows the word in use in 1440 and defines it as 'a semi-solid glutinous substance prepared from materials similar to those which furnish glue and used to mix with colours to dress cloth or paper etc'.

SLEY

Sometimes slay, in other words the loom reed. The word derives from the old English 'sleye', meaning a stroke. The alternative word, reed, derives from the material used to make the sley. Today both words are used almost indiscriminately.

SLUBBING

The web of well-open fibres removed from the cards which has to be divided into separate lengths, known by various names by various sections of the trade. Baines called them cardings or slivers, and sometimes slubbings. In any case, as he stated, these pieces or lengths of wool were converted into continuous lengths of sliver —Baines says yarn, but that is not really correct, since yarn is the finished product of the spinning. These slubbings were produced on a machine called the billy, and the people in charge of it were called slubbers; those employed under them were known as billy-boys, and were notoriously ill-treated.

The billy was an interesting machine, deriving from Hargreaves's 'Spinning Jenny', and played an important part in woollen-yarn production prior to the coming of the condenser.

SPINNERS AND PIECERS

When self-acting mules were introduced into the mills the normal custom in Yorkshire was to have a man spinner and a woman piecer for each pair of mules, and this has remained common practice today. It is perhaps worth noting that in the West of England we have always had one man spinner overlooking six to nine mules and a woman piecer on each mule.

TAMMIES

A cloth woven with a worsted weft and cotton warp, dyed fancy colours and highly glazed. Heaton said: 'By 1750 the industry was wide spread throughout the West Riding and Shalloons, Caliman-coes, Tammies, Camlets, etc., were made as far east as Leeds and Wakefield'.

There was a Tammy Hall at Wakefield; the second cloth hall built there, in 1766, was erected for the sale of this type of worsted and a considerable trade was done every Friday. Heaton notes that it had fallen into disuse by 1830.

TUNERS

Loom overlookers, or perhaps better described as loom engineers. With the hand loom, various jobs were done by the weaver—the setting up, the removal of the piece from the loom, as well as much else that has never been done by the tuner; the warping, for example.

When the weaving moved into the factories, the men who went in were at first in most cases expected to do the tuning themselves, but when women weavers were used (and this was the more common) men tuners were introduced, each being put in charge of a dozen or more looms. Gradually the division of labour was also applied when men weavers were employed, although it has remained a tradition that the man weaver will do certain jobs, mainly of relatively heavy nature like moving pieces out of the loom, which a woman weaver could not be expected to do.

TWILLS

The most important group of weaves. The common (2/2) are important for colouring: the glen, shepherd, gun club, pick and pick, etc for tartans and distinctive checks. The prunelle and other simple twills are not so widely used. But there are important fancy twills, the cavalry (or tautz) twill for example.

WATERLOOS

Presumably a fabric made to celebrate the famous victory.

WILDBORES

The *Oxford English Dictionary* gives this as a local word (1784-origin unknown) for a stout and closely woven, unglazed tammy.

APPENDIXES

ONE   From Daniel Defoe's *Tour Of Great Britain* (1724-6)

TWO   From Joseph Lawson's *Progress In Pudsey During the Last Sixty Years* (1887)

These two accounts of the Yorkshire wool-textile trade supplement Baines.

Defoe's account is of course well known, but his brilliant description of the sale on the bridge compares so well with what Baines says of the cloth halls that it deserves reprinting here.

The other extract is less well known. Though W. C. Crump used Lawson for his book and quoted some passages, the account is so good that more deserves reprinting. Its accuracy will be vouched for by all who have studied the trade. My own grandmother, one of the last hand-loom weavers in the west, often talked and complained of the unpleasantness of the wetting of the weft. I hope sufficient has been given to tempt all interested in the Yorkshire woollen and worsted trade to get this delightful but rare volume. I have made à few minor alterations to the text.

APPENDIX ONE

DEFOE'S DESCRIPTION OF THE WEST RIDING

The trade having been prodigiously encouraged and increased by the great demand of their Kerseys for clothing the armies abroad, in so much that it is the opinion of some that know the town and its bounds very well, that the number of people in the vicarage of Halifax, is increased one fourth, at least, within the last forty years, that is to say, since the last revolution. Nor is it improbable at all for besides the number of houses are increased they have entered upon a new manufacture, which was never made in those parts before, at least, not in any quantity, I mean, the manufacture of Shalloons, of which they now make, if fame does not belie them, a hundred thousand pieces a year in this parish only, and yet do not make much fewer Kerseys than they did before.

The trade in Kerseys also was so great, that I was told by very creditable, honest men when I was there, men not given to gasconading or boasting, and less to lying, that there was one dealer in the vicarage who traded by commission, for three-score thousand pounds a year in Kerseys only, and all that to Holland and Hamburg.

But not to enter into particulars, it is evident that the trade must be exceeding great, in that it employs such a very great number of people, and that in this one town only; for, as I shall fully describe in my account of other places, this is not what I may call the eldest son of the clothing trade in the county; the town of Leeds challenges a pre-eminence, and I believe merits the dignity it claims, besides the towns of Huddersfield, Bradford, Wakefield and others.

[Defoe then gives his own account of the well-known gibbet law.]

When this trade began to settle, nothing was more frequent than for young work-men to leave their cloths out all night upon tenters, and the idle fellows would come in upon them, and tearing them off without notice, steal the cloth. Now, as it was absolutely essential to preserve the trade in its infancy this severe law was made, giving the power of life and death so far in to the hands of the magistrates of Halifax, as to see the law executed upon them. As the law particularly pointed against the stealing of cloth, and no other crime, so no others were capable of being punished by it, and the conditions of the law intimate as much; for the power was not given to the magistrate to give sentence unless in one of these three plain cases :

(1) Hand Napping, that is, to be taken in the very fact or, as the Scots call it in the case of murder, Red Hand.
(2) Back Bearing, that is, when the cloth was found on the person carrying it off.
(3) Tongue Confessing, that part needs no further explanation.

They tell us of a custom which prevailed here, in the case of a criminal being to be executed, that if after his head was laid down, and the signal given to pull out the pin, he could be so nimble as to snatch out his head beneath the putting of the pin and the falling of the axe, and could get up on his feet, jump off the scaffold, run down a hill that lies just before it, and get through the river before the executioner could overtake him, and seize upon him, he was to escape; and although the executioner did take him on the other side of the river he was not to bring him back, at least he was not to be executed.

[Defoe then went to Leeds.]

A large wealthy and populous town, it stands on the north banks of the river Aire, is rather on both sides of the river for there is a large suburb or part of the town on the south side of the river, and the whole is joined by a stately and prodigiously strong stone bridge, so large, and so wide that formerly the cloth market was held in neither part of the town, but on the very bridge itself; and therefore the refreshment given the clothiers by the innkeepers of which I shall presently speak is called the brigg-shot to this day.

The increase of the manufacturers, and of the trade, soon made the market too great to be confined to the brigg or bridge, and it is now kept in the High Street begining from the bridge, and running up north almost to the market house. . . .

. . . The cloth market I am now to describe which is indeed a prodigy of its kind and is not equalled in the world. The market for serges at Exeter is indeed a wonderful thing, and the value sold there is very great; but then the market there is but once a week, here it is twice a week, and the quantity of goods is vastly great too.

The market itself is worth describing, though no description can come up to the thing itself; however take a sketch of it with its customs and usage as follows:

The street is a large, broad, fair and well-built street, beginning as I have said at the bridge and ascending gently to the north.

Early in the morning, there are trestles placed in two rows in the street, sometimes two rows on a side, but always one row at least;

168

then there are boards laid cross those trestles, so that the boards lie like long Counters on either side, from one side of the street to the other. The Clothiers come early in the morning with their cloth, and as few clothiers bring more than one piece, the market being so frequent, they go into the inns and public houses with it, and set it down.

At seven o'clock in the morning, the clothiers being supposed to have all come by that time, even in the winter, but the hour is varied as the season advances (in the summer earlier, in the depth of winter a little later) I take it at a medium, and it was when I was there, at six or seven, I say, the market bell rings; it would surprise a stranger to see in how few minutes without hurry or noise, and not the least dis-order, the whole market is filled; all the boards upon the trestles are covered with cloths, close to one another and as the pieces can lie long ways by one another, and behind every piece of cloth, the clothiers standing to sell it.

This indeed is not so difficult, when we consider that the whole quantity is brought into the market as soon as one piece, because as the clothiers stand ready in the inns and shops just behind, and that there is a clothier to every piece, they have no more to do, but like a regiment drawn up in line, everyone takes up his place, and has about five steps to march to lay it upon the first row of boards, and perhaps ten to the second row; so that upon the market bell ringing, in half a quarter of an hour the whole market is filled, the rows of boards covered and the clothiers stand ready.

As soon as the bell has done ringing, the merchants and factors and buyers of all sorts, come down, and coming along the spaces between the row of boards, they walk up the rows and down as their occasion directs. Some of them have their foreign letters of orders, with patterns sealed on them, in rows, in their hands; and with those they match colours, holding them to the cloths as they think they agree to; when they see any cloth to their colours, or that suit their occasions, they reach over to the clothier and whisper, and in the fewest words imaginable the price is stated; one asks, the other bids, and it is agree, or not agree, in a moment.

The merchants and buyers generally walk down and up twice on each side of the rows, and in little more than an hour all the business is done; in less than half an hour you will perceive the cloth begin to move off, the clothier taking it upon his shoulder to carry it to the merchants house; and by half an hour after eight o'clock the market bell rings again; immediately the buyers disappear, the cloth is all sold, or if here and there a piece happens not to be bought, it is carried back into the inn, and in a quarter of an hour, there is not a piece of cloth to be seen in the market.

Thus you see, ten or twenty thousand pounds value of cloth, and sometimes much more, bought and sold in little more than an hour and the laws of the market the most strictly observed that ever I saw done in any market in England; for—

(1)   Before the market bell rings, no man shows a piece of cloth, nor can the clothiers sell any but in the open market.
(2)   After the market bell rings again, nobody stays a moment in the market, but carries his cloth back if it be not sold.
(3)   And that which is most admirable, it is all managed with the most profound silence, and you cannot hear a word spoken in the whole market, I mean, by the persons buying and selling; it is all done in a whisper.

The reason of this silence, is chiefly because the clothiers stand so near to one another; and it is always reasonable that one should not know what another does, for that would be discovering their business, and exposing it to another.

If a merchant has bidden a clothier a price, and he will not take it, he may go after him to his house, and tell him he has considered it and is willing to let him have it; but they are not to make any new agreement for it, so as to remove the market from the street to the merchant's house.

By nine o'clock the boards are taken down, the trestles are removed, and the streets cleared, so that you see no market or goods any more than if there had been nothing to do; and this is done twice a week. By this quick returns the clothiers are constantly supplied with money, their work-men are duly paid and a prodigious sum circulates through the county every week.

[It was of course this cloth market that was so soon to lead to the famous cloth halls which continued to provide exactly the same service as Defoe describes. He goes on to question where all these cloths go. There are, he explains, really three ultimate customers. First of all the home consumers.]

The ordinary people, who cannot go to the price of fine medley cloths made in the western counties of England. There are, for this purpose, a set of travelling merchants in Leeds, who go all over England with droves of pack horses, and to all the fairs and market towns over the whole island, I think I may say none excepted. Here they supply not the common people by retail, which would denominate them pedlars indeed, but they supply the shops by wholesale or whole pieces; and not only so, but give large credit too, so that they are really travelling merchants, and as such they sell a very large quantity of goods; it is ordinary for one of these men to carry a thousand pounds value of cloth with them at a time, and having sold it at fairs or towns where they go, they send their horses back for as much more, and this very often in the summer, for they choose to travel in the summer, and perhaps towards winter time, though as little in winter as they can because of the badness of the roads.

Other sorts of buyers are those who buy to send to London; either by commission from London, or they give commissions to factors and warehouse keepers in London to sell for them; and these drive also a very great trade : These factors and warehouse keepers not only supply all the shop keepers and whole sale men in London, but sell also very great quantities to the merchants, as well for exportation to the English Colonies in America, which takes off great quantities of these coarse goods, especially New England, New York, Virginia, etc., as also to the Russian merchants, who send an exceeding quantity to Petersburg, Riga, Danzig, Narva, and to Sweden and Pomerania.

The third sort of buyer who are not less considerable than the others, are truly merchants, that is to say, such as receive commissions from abroad to buy cloth for the merchants chiefly in Hamburg, and in Holland and from several other parts; and these are not only many in number, but some of them are very considerable in their dealings, and correspond as far as Nuremburg, Frankfurt, Leipsig and even to Vienna and Augsburg in the farthest province of Germany.

APPENDIX TWO

From J. Lawson's *Progress In Pudsey* (Letter 6)

What is the chief employment—weaving cotton on hand looms—power looms supersede them—making of woollen cloths—hand looms, jennies etc.—lead houses and wool dyeing—drying wool and tentering pieces out of doors—moiting wool by hand—lecking pieces—cloth makers go to the Leeds market—their talk at the inns on the road—wetting bobbins with a sahker—revolution caused by the bobbin sinker—hand loom weaving has its drawbacks.

Sixty years ago in passing through the villages of Pudsey, especially the upper part of it, we hear slight but rapid tappings or rappings in the houses made by the flying shuttles of the hand loom weavers of cotton. There are also some weaving worsteds; though we are not aware that any of the cotton manufacturers reside in the village the warps are put out by agents and the pieces are taken in and paid for by them. The weavers in some cases are men, but mostly women, girls and boys, and the looms may be seen in the houses where they live as we pass along. But we soon see these cotton looms taken down, and in most cases hand looms for weaving woollen cloths put in their places. The making of woollen cloth has long been the chief employment of the villages, though of a crude sort of cloth. In the cotton branch power looms are superseding the hand looms, in spite of the determined opposition of the hand loom weavers, who at Blackburn destroyed more than a thousand in one week and at Shipley a power loom for weaving worsteds is dragged through the streets and destroyed. The cloth made at this time in Pudsey is mostly made of coarse wool, thick-spun and woven in an open set of gears and slays. In Leeds a finer wool is made up into better cloth, though Leeds is noted for its stuff manufacturers, whose merchants attend the Bradford and Halifax markets to sell their goods. It is not long since the picking stick and flying shuttles were introduced. Our fathers tell us of seeing persons throw the shuttles with their hands through the shed or sheard, or of two persons when the cloth was broader weaving on one loom. They also tell us of seeing carding done by hand, and the yarn being spun a single thread at a time on the spinning wheel. There are spinning jennies now, one with fifty spindles is considered a great affair; there are many with thirty eight spindles and we have spun on one of that count for days together nearly twenty years after the time we are speaking of. Nearly sixty years ago some of the people walked to Bramley, Armley, Farnley and Wortly, back-wards and forwards every day, to weave or spin; others work at manufacturers houses in the village; while others have looms in the chamber over where they live and get work from makers in slubb-ing coppings, from the slubbers at the mills which they draw out on the jennies into warp and weft and weave into cloth on their hand looms.

The cloth makers are a hard working resolute sort of folk, and we have heard one tell how he had fetched a pack of wool on his back from Halifax and litted it, that is dyed it the same day; and that it was not uncommon for persons to do it. Places for dyeing, called lead houses, are to be seen throughout the villages and many woollen manufacturers have one on their own premises. The wool is mostly dried out of doors, as are cloths on tenters. When the spinning jennies were first introduced you should have been there, and seen and heard the people or some of them, the more conserva-tive sort of folks who always dread a change. They are lamenting and downcast: 'England is ruined, one man will do the work of ten and get very little more for it', they say, and that there will not be half work for the people in the future. At first all yarns were spun into coppings, the weft about half the twist of the warp, and the former is still wound on to bobbins on the one spindled wheel ready for the weavers shuttle, and we have seen the winders who are mostly women, girls and boys, with the blood dropping off their fingers caused by the friction of the yarn in winding these bobbins. In a while we see a great change. Wires are put round the jenny spindles to hold the bobbins by the staples and prevent them being loose and to make them go round with the spindle, and thus supersedes the winding on the bobbin wheel. Then we hear of another general outcry made, and what with one thing or another there is going to be nothing to do for people soon but to pine (starve) to death. There are some who after all stick to the winding on the wheel, their fathers and mothers had done so and it must be best. A time comes, however, when they give away and acknowledge the jenny an institution which is quite constitutional.

Some of the wool used has many burrs and moits (as motes are called) in it, and a large number of women and children fetch it a stone at a time to moit, for there are no burring or moiting machines to take them out. Weavers have to wet or leck the piece when woven by putting on a liquid to scour or wash out the grease etc. at the mill, and it is quite common to see weavers carry these pieces full of not very sweet liquid on their backs or in a wheelbarrow. It requires a rather expensive plant for a poor weaver to prepare the liquid required, but they lend and borrow amongst each other.

The poor were poorer then than now, so that a man, who could make as much cloth as employed his one own family only would be considered rich. There is a deep meaning in this idea, and much truth, for what independance man feels when he can employ himself and not be compelled to ask another for work to enable him to live. Seeking and asking, and almost begging and praying for work to save one from starvation is one of the most humiliating sights one can imagine, and we have known persons whose greatest ambition was to be a woollen manufacturer in order to be able to employ himself and his family, so as to be saved from the degradation of asking others not only his equals but in many cases far below him in everything that constitutes good character to allow him to live. Many of these old time clothiers are men of this sort, and only make sufficient to employ themselves and families. Some have a few outside looms, but there are few large manufacturers; and many now with the great production power they possess—the result of the many improvements in machinery during even the last thirty years—are able to make as much profit from their large production or turnover in almost any year as our old manufacturers would have made if the cost of all they manufactured had been profit!

Before concluding this letter we will refer to a matter which some may think is of small importance, but it is really a most momentous one, trivial as some may think it, involving on a small scale quite a revolution in connection with the business of a hand loom weaver, viz., that of: *wetting bobbins*.

The loose fibres of the weft prevented it coming off the bobbins in going across the warp, except it was wet with water, which was also necessary to enable the weaver to get his weft 'in' by making the shots called shoot lay closer to each other to make a fine cloth. Each bobbin of weft had to be thoroughly soaked in water; after which a number of them were piled on each other in what was called a 'siper' to drain the bulk of the water off. This siper was made in the form of a V. The old mode of wetting bobbins was as follows: The weaver had a bowl or some other vessel of water under the siper, into which he put his bobbin, and taking one at a time he held it under the water with his left hand, having in his right hand a wooden tube called a 'bobbin sahker', meaning sucker, to which he applied his mouth, placing the lower end of the tube close against the weft on the bobbin under water and then sucked or withdrew the air, so as to cause the water to thoroughly soak the weft; but if from mismanagement the tube was not placed perfectly in the bobbin the dirty water would rush into the weaver's mouth, which was a common occurrance, and what made this an aggravated calamity was that sometimes very disagreeable ingredients were in the bobbin water, from which arose an offensive odour. Then in winter time the water was frequently either frozen or within a few degrees of frost, when the process with one hand in the water was performed, which made it a cold job.

Well there came a time which produced quite a revolution in the mode of wetting bobbins. Someone invented an instrument to supersede the 'bobbin sahker', for from time immemorial there have been men who were not satisfied with things as they were, especially if they got it into their heads that things as they were could be improved. This has always been the case, and probably always will be to the end of time. This new invention was not called a 'bobbin sahker' because it was not one, but a bobbin sinker which it was. It was founded on the principle of a pump or a boys squirt, made of tin, and so shaped at the bottom end as to cover the bobbin of weft, which was held under water, and the air was displaced by pulling up a wooden stopper wrapped with weft to fill the tin tube, by which simple process the bobbin of weft was saturated with water. There was great rejoicing by men of progress when they first saw this bobbin sinker, for in it they saw a great deliverance from considerable difficulty and annoyance caused by the old 'bobbin sahker'. But here again was manifested the old conservative element, persons opposed to all change except the raising of weaving a penny or twopence per string. They protested against the newfangled notion of a bobbin sinker and struck to the old 'sahker' as they probably would to their mother's breast had they been allowed to do so. These went on in the old way until they either died off or sulkily took to the new improvements for wetting bobbins.

Hand loom weavers, with a good warp and a good weft and not too much of the latter is put in, with constant work and double the price they got for weaving, would not be an objectionable business. The weaver was under shelter and not exposed as some out-of-door labourers were. Weavers had much freedom, could work short hours and make it up when convenient, not being called to labour by a bell. But the hand-loom weaver had many drawbacks and many difficulties, and trials, and much tribulation, as we shall try to show in our next article.

Letter 7

The Trials and Difficulties of Hand Loom Weavers

Cloth makers become numerous—panics and bad times—small manufacturers—few weavers and spinners have constant work—seeking work—bad customs, 'odd jobbing' or working for nothing—waiting for slubbing—sizing and 'laking for druft'—putting webs out to dry—seeking gears—power looms dreaded—effects of machinery—open band and cross band—difficulty in making cloths alike.

176

From the time of which we have been speaking, the population of Pudsey continued to increase, and small woollen manufacturers became more numerous, when a different class of goods began to be made in a greater variety, but much less durable in weaving, finer spun, and woven in finer gears and slays. Amongst all the changes, or mixed up with them, both in the old and new state of things, there were bad times, when the working classes were sorely tried and at their 'wit's end' to get sufficient porridge and bread. With all our present 'depressed trade' we know comparatively nothing of what the people experienced in what some foolishly call the 'good old times'. Were it within our present province it would be easy to write a good sized volume on the continually recurring panics and bad times, such as when the manufacturers of Huddersfield told Parliament that thirteen thousand people in the fancy trade were working for $2\frac{1}{2}$d. per day, and paying for the wear and tear of their looms out of it! The suffering of the people, not only in Pudsey but in almost every part of the country, both in the various manufacturing and the agricultural districts, was beyond all adequate description during the first half of the present century.

But apart from these frequent times of acute suffering, this change in the class of woollen goods made at Pudsey did not, in the best of times, make it a matter for the hand loom weavers to get along; they had many trials and difficulties to contend with. There were few who could depend on constant work (even when trade was not bad) from any of the manufacturers. Of course there were a few of the largest makers who were able to supply something like regular work, but such cases were rare. Few weavers knew when they got a piece to make for whom they would be spinning and weaving the next.

The bad customs we may enumerate in connection with cloth making were more common, we believe, in the upper part of the village than in the lower, although far too prevalent in all parts. The manufacturers being mostly small capitalists, had often to sell one lot before they could make another, being, as it were said, 'from hand to mouth'. Some of them would frankly tell their men this, and urge them on, so that they might be able to buy more wool and the men have more work. It was quite common when trade was not bad to see weavers and spinners going from place to

177

M

place seeking work, or to get a piece of cloth to make. If they succeeded it was mostly on the condition that they helped to break the wool for it; that is open the bale, then the fleece taking off the coarse parts called the britch, put it in sheets, then go to the mill and help to scour it, then 'lit' or dye it and the morning after take it out of the dyepans into sheets ready for the dryhouse. If to dye black, then the wool had to be scoured, that is a foundation for the colour given it ready for dyeing the day following. All this was for nothing, except in some cases a small allowance for a little ale or cheese and bread. If the wool was taken to Leeds to dye indigo blue, then it was only to open and britch and to be looked over, that is, all the white bits taken out, or lumps of tar cut off locks, when it comes from the dyehouse. However, after doing all this work the weaver did feel somewhat relieved, knowing he had a claim now to a share in working it up when he could get a set of slubs to be spinning a web on the jenny. The small manufacturer sometimes put all the blend out in single pieces, that is single webs (but mostly in cloths, two web lots) as he wanted to have the cloth as soon as possible to market. When the slubber had doffed the first set of slubbing, it often became a serious question as to whose turn it was to have it, and casting lots would frequently be the mode of deciding it, for it was common for several weavers and spinners to be there waiting for it, and sometimes all the slubbing for the warps would be fetched from the mill in odd sets as doffed. Probably the weaver would be waiting for the warp being spun for his web, or the warper for the warp to warp. All this working for nothing and waiting took up time while rents, rates, coal and grocery bills were being run up. Then lists for the cloth's selvedge had to be laid at the master's house, and sometimes there was waiting there either for the listing or their turn at the bartrees. When the webs were warped there was the sizing process to go through, and the weavers as a rule had to bring their own size, though customs varied very much with different manufacturers in the village—there was nothing like uniformity in either wage or customs, which was a great drawback to both weavers and spinners. Well, the weavers might have to wait for his size at the sizing boilers, and the size varied in strength, or if not the webs varied in their taking or absorbing it, and it was common for weavers to ask advice from their neighbours,

178

and sometimes a little Size Conference might be seen deliberating as to which size pot would be safest to pull the web through; while at other times if there was no suitable pot, or the web was very tender, the weavers would wring the size out of the webs (after possing it) with his hands—rather tedious work, and requiring good judgment to do it all alike. This sizing business was an important affair, for on it being done properly or otherwise most serious results depended. If a web got a soft size, that is too little in it, the warp would chafe in the gears and slays, and flour was sometimes put on to make it work; while, if too hard-sized, water had to be spurted on to it behind the gears.

After sizing the web, one of the most critical of all the processes is to put it out of doors to dry, for in a climate like ours the weather, especially at some seasons, is very fickle. A place is chosen, the web-sticks or stretchers are put out, and if frosty, a pickaxe is used to make holes in the ground for posts to hold the ends of the web, and a maul to drive them down. Sometimes might be seen a man and his wife up to their knees in snow going out with a web to dry, she carrying the web sticks and her husband the wet web. This reminds one of a lecturer coming up, we think it was Swinnow; the woman was carrying the web sticks, etc., which are not very easy for a woman to carry, and someone shouted out to him 'Hey'er em, wi'tah'; the stranger, a highly educated man, wished to know the meaning of the expression, and was much amused when told it meant 'carry them for her wilt thou'.

Well, in winter time and when fine weather is scarce, webs get only partly dried and have to be hung before the house or stove fire to finish; but it is quite a common thing to see a number of weavers who say they are 'laking for druft', that is waiting for fine weather to dry their webs. Yes, 'druft', as it was called, was a most momentous matter with the hand loom weavers. The next thing was the sort of gear and slay he must have, and owing to the sets having begun to vary so much it was seldom that the same set could be used many times in succession. Gears and slays were rather expensive for a weaver, and they had mostly to find their own; therefore there was much lending and borrowing of gears. It was a common thing to see weavers, who had been for hours, and in some cases, a day or two trying to borrow gears, five, six and some odd times it might be a seven portif quarter gear, nine to ten or eleven quarters wide, etc., as the case happened to be. Part Spanish wool was used, which had many burrs in it and a deal of what was called moity work was the result. Australian wool had not come fairly into use for woollens then, and these burrs, etc., gave the weavers much trouble and having but a very bad light, there being no gas still, candles and oil lamps were used, some preferring the one and some the other. Often might be seen a boy or girl, or perhaps a weaver's wife, standing on one side of the loom watching to see when a thread broke down whilst the weaver watched the other side, because if a thread broke and another 'shoit' was picked a dozen more might be broken. Then there was much poor work caused by uneven slubbing, which made a bad thread; by 'twitty' warp, that is the thread having very small places in it which soon broke : caused also sometimes by spinning smaller or finer than the quality of the wool warranted; besides burry wool would prevent the weft from coming off the bobbins and gave the weavers trouble. The overlookers who scribbled and carded the wool often spoiled it and many weavers as well as masters had to suffer for that. Let us now suppose that the weaver has felled, that is finished weaving the web. The next thing to be done was to leck or wet it as before explained, ready for a carrier to take it to the mill to be scoured. When fulled or milled as they called it, there was the tentering. Probably now it would be done in the tenter-house, which was made almost as hot as an oven, if on the days before Leeds market, and when dried the cloth had to be 'teemed', which means being taken off and laid on the grass to get the dew and pulled along to clean it to give a proper handle or touch to the merchants. The night might be in winter, cold and chilly, especially to persons who had come out of the hot tenter-house. After standing out with the cloth a proper time to catch sufficient dew it had to be listed and cuttled and put under a weight ready for the carrier taking it to Leeds market the following day. Many cases of sickness occurred amongst the weavers and some deaths caused by this exposure in dewing cloth. All this odd obbing we say was done for nothing, and the wages paid for weaving and spinning alone without doing all this at the bargain, were very poor indeed. Some said that if these bad customs went on at the rate they had done, getting worse and worse every year, in the end weavers would have to find the manufacturers headings, lists and gig bits before they could get a piece to make, and if some in our day think that hand loom weavers have not sufficient tribulations in those days, we have only to say to such that had they been compelled to do what these weavers did their opinions would have been considerably modified. In addition to all this, what was called 'outside makers' had considerable expense in the first outlay of looms, jennies and bartrees, etc., such as shuttles, pickers and all wear and tear as well as rent for the loom, light and fuel in winter. Some of these 'outside makers', that is persons who had looms at home and got slubbing to make up for the masters, had four looms and it took the principle nearly all his time to do the odd jobbing for them, and we cannot wonder that a hand loom weaver came to be called a poverty knocker. It was no uncommon thing to do, when the work was done, for the weaver to be unable to get paid for some time after, which often caused much disappointment, inconvenience and suffering. As to the price paid for weaving and spinning, some idea may be got from the fact that certain classes of goods were made called petershams, for which only 21/- —and in some cases only £1—was paid, for fetching the slubbing from the mills, spinning it into warp and weft, warping the web, sizing, looming and weaving it into cloth, which in many cases took a man a fortnight to accomplish. Such was the conditions of things, so when power looms first began to be introduced, and which many were lamenting and complaining, we always said things could not well be worse, and that there was one consolation, power looms could not break the wool nor seek work, nor scour, dye, fetch slubbing, warp lists, size and dry webs, seek gears or pay for them, leck pieces and carry them to the mill, tenter, 'teem' or dew and cuttle them. We said we wished everything was done by power or machinery from dyeing, selling and designing, to book-keeping, so that the people had nothing to do but read, think, write and study nature, sketch or draw, travel and re-create themselves by some rational and innocent amusement, for that even then the masses of the people at that time could hardly help getting a better share in the distribution of wealth as machinery could not eat or drink all it produced, nor could a few capitalists. We still believe there is some truth in this, if not strictly so, and that just in proportion as machinery is adopted, though during the transition people whose labour is superseded will suffer more or less, ultimately will society be bencfited and get a large share of needful things, though it may not be a proportionate share with the large capitalists, who may be able to rapidly heap up large fortunes. It may easily be seen that the above rude, unjust and oppressive customs were penny wise and pound foolish, for the work done for nothing could not be possibly done, particularly some of it, as well as if done by men, specially devoting all their time to such, as came to be the case ultimately.

In concluding this letter, it may not be amiss to mention a few difficulties and inconveniences to which both masters, spinners and weavers were subject. All work was put out to make in a certain number of warterns of slubbing for each two or four ends of cloth. A wartern meant 6 lbs. and if a blend of wool yielded less weight of slubbing than was expected it was a serious matter for a small manufacturer, making sometimes all the difference of a profit or loss. Hence such were very anxious about the yield of slubbing, and an old friend of mine tells a story in his own experiences as to what happened when he first began to make cloth himself. He was much disappointed in the weight of slubbing he got, it being much less than he expected, and on Sunday, though a very devout Methodist at the time in spite of all he could do during singing, praying and the sermon, this short weight constantly forced itself in his mind. During all that Sunday, whatever he might be doing and wherever he might be, there rang in his ears his short weight, which if we remember rightly was twenty six warterns and two pounds. Yes, the weight of the slubbing was a most important consideration, and liable to upset all previous calculations, for short weight meant fewer strings and fewer yards of cloth to sell. Spinners had often to stop spinning warp until the weight of slubbing could be ascertained or bribes had to be made which was quite common. This meant that a different kind of weft had to be used to fell or finish the webs. These bribes were quite common; and many persons, mostly manufacturers, might be seen with one thrown over their shoulder as a substitute for overcoats, even when going to the Leeds market.

Again under the old system of jennies and hand looms, cloth could not be made as uniform. If the work was not so good a spinner would perhaps spin the warp thicker to make a stronger thread, and would have less weft which he might spin a little smaller or finer. Sometimes the web was warped a portiff or two narrower to make up for the thick spinning; and if one weaver acted according to orders and another took liberties the ends would not mill together in the stock; one yielding broader or shorter than the other. Then some spinner would give his warp more twist than another, and similarly with the weft, and this would affect the milling or fulling in the stocks.

After a while the manufacturers had the slubbing for warp twisted one way and that for the weft its opposite called cross band and open band. It was a nice point to spin the exact amount for a web without having a little left or being a little short—for one spinner would spin yarn that would yield more length to the skein than another, and it was common to have a little warp left or to be a little short, and have to spin to make out from the weft slubbing, and mix it with the other. This caused the weaver some trouble in tying threads up when they broke to use the proper kind of twist, which if not warped into the web properly showed itself and was a defect. Both warp and weft were often left, and from fear of the consequences if carried back to the manufacturers men were under some temptation to sell or make away with it while some would save it till short and use it when practicable. For all these various causes and many more, which might be enumerated, it will be seen that making cloths uniform was next to impossible, and where merchants weighed the pieces as well as measured, not only the length but the width as well, manufacturers at that day had much to contend with.

Letter 8

Burling and Burlers

Moity wools—burling cloths—great losses sustained—what burling is and who does it—dark weather—a bad scour—a great institution—burlers knew all and more—listeners at a burling house door—slubbers and their business —ill usage and poor pay for piecers—slubbers earn good wages and most of them spent it—condensers supersedes slubbing. Prejudice against them—false prophecies—America ahead of England—condensers hold their own, and slubbing dies out.

Any remarks dealing with the manufacture of woollen cloths would be deficient if nothing was said about burlers and burling. Old manufacturers know what an important branch or department this was for fifty down even to thirty years ago. Large numbers of women and girls were burlers of cloth.Australian and Cape wools were in course of time brought into general consumption and these wools were in a bad condition compared with what they are today although with the present means of destroying vegetable matter in wools, and of taking out the old pests of burrs and moits, it ceases to be such a nuisance as then. Fifty years ago there were many blues, blacks, browns, clarets and greens made and every colour had their various shades as well. After they were sold in the bulk, that is unfinished, by the manufacturer to the Leeds merchants, they were sent to the finisher, who raised and cut them to gain a face on them, so that every speck in the clock was laid bare and if the cloths were not clean burled, they were damaged or imperfect goods. All who are likely to see our remarks will know what we mean by burling, and it is therefore only necessary to say that when the cloth was scoured so as to show all the burls (specks), a burler's business was to pick these out with small irons, which had fine points, and could be easily and rapidly closed so as to pull the speck out. During dark weather or if the cloth was not properly cleaned in the scouring it would probably prove burly and much of the cloth made was very bad to make free from burls. This department often gave great trouble and anxiety to the manufacturer, lest cloths should either not be properly done or cost too much doing, for thousands of pounds had been deducted from what manufacturers expected to realise owing to burly cloths. It was customary for the merchant to see how the cloths proved with regard to burls before they paid for them or to pay something on account, stopping a balance till the goods were finished.

This burling was a great institution of itself formerly. Scores of women and younger girls might be seen going to and fro fetching ends on their shoulders to burl, or taking them back when done. Many manufacturers had burling houses or sheds with several boards or tables to work on; others put their burling out. Some burlers hired burling sheds, and got work out where they could; while many burled at their own houses. There was much difference in burlers: some were quick, some were slow, some reliable, others not. All the burled ends of cloth had to be perched to see whether they were clean. Some would be only a few minutes in passing satisfactorily while others were always a long time, having to be re-burled on the perch. It was amusing to listen outside the burling house when a few burlers were at work. They knew all that is passing in the villages, what the people are doing and saying, who had just begun the business, who are intending to begin; who wants but cannot succeed, who have broken off their engagements, and why; the faults if not the virtues of all; what births have taken place; what are going to take place; the christenings, weddings and deaths. They knew people's circumstances; how much some owed to the grocers, and what some wanted to owe, and how courteously, or it might be roughly and rudely, they were prevented. They knew how persons were dressed last Sunday, and how they will be dressed next; the latest style and fashion, the cost of nearly every bonnet, shawl and dress. Then the burlers attend various churches or chapels and sometimes in passing a few boards of burlers you would be apt to think there was either a concert or some religious service going on. They knew all the last Whitsuntide school tunes, and most of the old substantial ones, such as Luther's hymns, etc. There is most exquisite harmony, and not a mere rehearsal, for they are singing daily. If these burlers had had a chance of a decent education, and had chosen to follow it up, the burling shed might have been a kind of college, there was very little noise caused by their work; so that they could converse freely and did so. Unfortunately there was much tittle tattle to be heard; backbiting and slander were too common. A burling house was something like an epitome of the world, where even the most virtuous had some faults and the worst had some redeeming qualities. But another distinct class were males, not females, and were called:

SLUBBERS.

These drew out the cardings, and wound them on to coppings as slubbings ready for the spinners to spin on their jennies. Slubbers could earn about twice as much as the hand loom weavers could, but paid the little boys and girls who were piecers (rubbing the

185

N

carding ends together) a very small pittance—only 3/- or 3/6d. for standing doing their work the whole week of sometimes 90 hours. Some of the slubbers behaved very badly to these young boys and girls, beating them most cruelly. In winter time fathers might be seen carrying their children on their backs by five o'clock in the morning through the deep snow to their work at the mills. Many with crooked legs might be seen—the result of standing fifteen, sometimes sixteen hours a day piecing. Though the slubbers could earn such good wages, yet as a class they were considered a drunken people, and somewhat extravagant in other respects. Probably working long hours tended to lure them to drink and excitement when not working, especially on Saturday nights and Sundays, as one extreme often produces another. Our remarks about the spare and scanty diet of the hand loom weavers will not apply to this class, except in cases where they wasted their wages by want of frugality. If a young woman was courted by a slubber she was looked upon as being fortunate. But the slubbers as a class were rather self conceited. They thought themselves much superior to hand loom weavers, and refused at times to sit and drink with the latter in the tap room and passed into the bar, where they drank spirits or from a superior tap of ale. We remember, however, it being a common remark that if a slubber fell short of funds towards the end of the week (as many of them frequently did) and wanted a loan till the wage day, he had to go to a hand loom weaver for relief, his fellow slubbers not being able to supply him. In course of time a terrible change took place for these proud slubbers—a machine was introduced which made the system of slubbing on what was called the billy useless; it was called:

THE CONDENSER.

from which came continuous threads of something like slubbing. Most of those likely to notice our letters will know what a condenser is; it dispensed with the old carding machines and billies.

The threads from the condenser were wound on to spools as they came from the machines and were then removed to a frame in front of the mule where the threads were spun into warp and weft as required. It must be understood that long before condensers were introduced spinning on the mule was common, which superseded the old spinning jenny (slubbings being spun by the mules) so that very few jennies were in use, but both the slubbers and the jenny spinners were now dispensed with. Dispensing with slubbing and slubbers were not all that was affected by the condensers. In the new process the fibre of the wool was placed lengthwise, which caused the thread to be much stronger. About forty years ago, whilst in America, we saw a condenser for the first time, and in the United States we found them almost everywhere. Every woollen manufacturer of any note had them, and we only saw after much travelling one billy for slubbing, and that was where only custom work was done, that is where farmers sent their wool to be made into such fabrics as they wished. Billies were confined to those out of the way places mostly, we are told, on streams with water power and one set of machines. We made enquiries about the condensers as to where they came from, and were told from Belgium and other countries on the continent of Europe; but at the time we are referring to they were made in the States. On our return to England we explained the condenser to manufacturers and spoke highly of them but were laughed at and told that they might do for America where everything was in such a rude state and where they did not understand their business; or they might suit worsted goods but would never do for woollens, because the chief object in carding would be defeated, as a full thread was wanted and not the fibres put lengthwise; that condensing would spoil fine cloths by making them hard; that the cloth would have no elasticity and would break like cotton goods, etc. We told them that French and Belgium goods were all condensed and were being bought in the United States in preference to the English goods; they, having a much higher finish and being twice or thrice as strong. After a long period a few condensers were introduced into Pudsey for warps, and then those conservative manufacturers said : 'Well, they may do for warps but never for wefts'. After a while they were used for wefts, and then it was said : 'Well, they may do for all wools but never for short stuffs such as mungo and shoddy'. We were telling this recently to a first rate scribbler and condenser called an overlooker. He laughed most heartily and pointing to a blend before us which was being condensed he asked : 'How could this job be done at all without a condenser?' and added: 'There is not a bit of pure wool in it, and no man on earth could card this blend so as to make a good yarn'. On looking at the thread on the bobbins after it had been spun we saw an even, smooth and strong thread of weft.

This shows that the United States of America were long ahead of us in the principle of condensing. Of course every slubber was certain that a condenser was an infamous imposition and would never act or answer the purpose, and most heartily hoped it would prove so. There was a little difficulty at first owing to the ignorance of those whose business it was to attend to them. If there are any old slubbers still living, they will never forget the era or first introduction of condensers, for they were glad to sit in the tap room or anywhere else after that with the hand loom weavers. The time for their humiliation had come, and it was pitiful to see some of the slubbers who, for some time, persisted in their assertion that condensers would soon all be thrown out and carding and slubbing be re-adopted, hanging about in a sad condition. Their voice soon got considerably weaker; the faith in billies the same; and unheeded condensers went on and prospered. Carding and slubbing are now things of the past. Some of the slubbers were too proud to do anything but slub. Others learnt to weave on the hand loom and others did anything they could. Machinery, when first introduced, was a very serious matter to those whose labour is thereby displaced. It is during the transition time that certain classes of labourers suffer, though ultimately it is a great benefit to society and the working people where the new machine is adopted and set to work. Before we were acquainted with the principle of condensing, the strength of the French and Belgium superfine cloths imported in America seemed unexplicable. We had imported some fine English black cloths but they were not comparable for strength. After seeing these (to us) new machines at work, and understanding the principle of them, the mystery was all cleared away and made patent to every man of common sense.

Letter 13

Contributory Causes of Change and Progress in the Manufacture of Woollens

Our purpose—what it is and what it is not—recapitulation of processes—Australian wool—its history—mungo—cotton warps—prediction falsified—piece dyeing—burl dyeing—fancy coatings—great increase in the number of woollen manufacturers—hawking cloth and cloth hawkers—many cloth makers begin to finish their goods—Leeds cloth hall is deserted and company mills decay.

In our letters 6, 7 and 8 we have already dealt briefly with the manufacture of the woollen cloths in Pudsey, promising to return to the subject later on . . .

At one time the one spindled bobbin wheel was seen to have been a most important machine until it was superseded by the spinning jenny which began to wind the weft it spun on to the bobbin, and the jenny itself, after being enlarged in its numbers of spindles was displaced by the mule. We endeavoured to represent old time cloth making and cloth makers as we remembered seeing them, with their notions, habits and customs of that day . . .

[Mentions the coming of Australian wools] : —
It is not eighty years since the first wool was brought to this country from New South Wales. In the year 1808 a Mr. Marsden brought ten or twelve stones to London and offered it to the well known Thompsons of Rawdon on condition that they would make it into cloth : they were to have it for nothing except paying the carriage from London . . .

This firm did so at the mill near where we write this; the cloth proved much better than expected. George III had a coat made of it.

Letter 14

Power Looms and the Revolution They Effected

No progress without decay—machinery and its effects—strong opposition to power looms—Blackburn, Bradford and Leeds—a curious petition to Parliament—the old hand loom weavers lament—'to be sold by auction'—great depreciation of values in property—'the darkest clouds have a silver lining'—manufacturers have to buy their own machinery and pay for all odd jobbings—the worsted business—etc.

It was some time before power looms for weaving woollen cloths were introduced, and then very slowly, though it was plain enough to all thoughtful minded people that the doom of hand looms was fixed. Many of the old weavers might be heard saying that power looms might do for narrow goods, such as cottons and stuffs, but never for broadcloths. Meanwhile, unheeded, power looms for weaving broadcloths steadily marched on, being introduced first by one large manufacturer and then another; and it was well for the hand loom weavers that the introduction was not more rapid or the shock and suffering for the time would have been more severe. Slubbers had been displaced, but they were not such a numerous class as the weavers. Spinners or jennies had been superseded by mule spinners, but many of them could weave and jennies were taken down and looms put up in their places, whilst some of the most skilful and enterprising learnt to spin on the mule. But when both billy, jenny and hand loom were rendered useless the old weavers saw nothing in the world worth living for, and began to feel there was nothing for them to do. The hand loom weavers formed a large class of men and women, as well as boys and girls in their teens. Many years before when cloths began to be made broader, the old ten and eleven quarter looms had been taken down and put on the 'balks' next to the roof, with a strong faith that before long they would be wanted again when the temporary whim was over. But that time never came, and the old looms lay piled there to rot (as cotton and worsted looms had done) and were ultimately used to light the fire or for other base uses never thought of by their once owners. But in the case of power looms it was not a question of width or strength of the hand looms, good, bad and indifferent were all the same. Power looms spoke as with a voice of thunder to all who had ears to hear: 'Get out of our way, ye have had your day, see the march of your superiors'.

The change had a terrible effect on the minds of some of the old hand loom weavers. Many an old weaver had become as much attached to his favourite loom as a warrior to his old steed, or the owner of 'Poor Dog Tray' to his dog. We have seen an old Pudsey weaver with tears in his eyes while looking at and recounting the good points of his loom. Yes, it was hung on its prods as a loom ought to be, and swung to and fro as a loom should do, the going part easy to put back yet came freely to its work, and would get any amount of weft in. When that loom first came from one of the best makers in England, all so smooth, sleek and trim, thirteen quarter wide—he was envied by all who saw it; the neighbours all came to see it, and admired and coveted it. But now for some time both the loom and another which is not to be despised, being much better than the average—together with a once famous jenny, bartree, creel and bobbin wheel—have all been dumb and covered with dust and cobwebs . . .

INDEX

Airedale, 46
Akroyd, Mr, 128
Alfred the Great, and clothmaking, 81
Almondbury, 17
Alpaca, raw material, 119, 129, 145; rise of industry, 130
Alverthorpe, 17
Angora, 132
Aniline dyes, introduction of, 133
Architecture, industrial, in Yorkshire, 30; Bean Ing Mill, 51, 52
Arkwright, Richard, 32, 39; and roller spinning, 41, 42, 46, 126
Armstrong, T., *Crowthers of Bankdam*, 61
Atkinson, F. C., *Some Aspects of Eighteenth Century Woollen & Worsted Trade in Halifax*, 59
Aulnage, account of West Riding, 18, 26; administration, methods of, 27; complaint against agents, 28, 56
Australia, merino wool, 88; import of wool, 89; importance of wool from, 108
Austria, 112

Baines, Edward, Jnr (1800-1890), MP for Leeds, letter from Gladstone, 8; *History of Cotton Manufacture in Great Britain*, 42
Baines, Edward, Snr (1774-1845), 7
Baker, Mr, factory inspector, 88, 91, 97, 99, 117; quoted, 138
Bakewell, Mr, sheep farming, 43
Bankfield Museum, Halifax, 37
Bar or Bartree, 145
Bates, Mr, factory inspector, 99
Batley, 97; shoddy first manufactured, 101, 102, 104, 111
Bays (also baize), 45, 145; manufacturers of, 87, 107
Bean Ing Mills, Leeds, mills of Mr Gott, 51; workers at, 53
Behrens, Mr, on worsted trade, 141
Belgium, 112
Bentley, Phyllis, 61
Beverley, medieval clothmaking at, 9; Law of Fullers and Weavers of,

10, 14, 15; Leland at, 18
Bichromate of potash (chrome), 145
Bickley, F., *Little Red Book of Bristol*, 55
Big Ben, Cartwright's combing machine, 54
Billy, machine in woollen-yarn manufacture, 13; wages of workers on, 93, 109
Bingley, 26, 27, 123, 135
Bischoff, James, 52; *History of Woollen and Worsted Industries*, 60; freeing imported wool from duty, 77
Blackwell Hall, 19
Blankets, exports of, 87
Boiling the cloth (roll boiling), 73
Bombazines, 130
Bourn, Daniel of Leominster, 32, 41
Brabant, 11
Bradford (Yorkshire), 17, 26, 27, 29, 46, 80, 82, 84; population of, 85; development of worsted trade, 122; Piece Hall at, 123; surpasses Halifax, 124; mohair industry, 132; worsted industry, 134
Bradley, T., architect, 57
Bristol, medieval clothmaking at, 9; guild regulations at, 13; size of cloth trade at, 19
Britch, type of wool, 146
British Association for the Development of Science, 67, 83
Broadcloth, 17, 146; decline of white broadcloth trade, 28, 29; superfine broadcloths in Yorkshire, 52; cost of manufacturing at Bean Ing, 53, 70
Brushing the cloth, 73
Budding, Mr, of Stroud, 47, 59
Burling, woollen process defined, 72; wages of workers, 108; description of, 146; in Pudsey, 183
Burnley, James, *History of Wool and Wool Combing*, 60
Burrs, fault in wool, 91, 147, 174

Calderdale, 46

192

Calemancoes, type of worsted cloth, 123, 147
Calverly, 17
Camblets (or Camblettes), type of worsted cloth, 44, 123, 148
Cambridge, choristers buy Yorkshire cloth, 19
Canterbury, worsteds at, 121
Carding, woollen process, 13, 14, 72; invention of rotary carding, 32, 36, 37, 69
Carpets, export of, 87
Cartwright, Edmund, inventor of power loom, 54, 128
Carus-Wilson, Professor E. M., 11, 55, 56; works by, 62
Cassimere, see Kerseymere
Castleford, 17
Challoner, W. H., note on Edward Baines, 6
Chester, 23
Child labour, in domestic industry and factory compared, 34; in factory, 137
China, export to, 113
Clapham, J. H., quoted, 44, 45
Cloth halls, 30; development in Yorkshire, 31; at Leeds, 99; Defoe's description of, 166
Clothiers, West of England and Yorkshire compared, 21; special position in West of England, 31; numbers of in United Kingdom, 90
Clothmaking, methods, 13-16
Clothworking, 15
Coburg, type of cloth, 148
Cockayne, Alderman, proposals on cloth trade, 24, 56
Colbert, French statesman, effect of policy on trade, 25
Colchester, worsted manufacture at, 121
Collier, J., inventor of combing machine, 48, 128
Colne, piece hall act, 123, 135
Combing, worsted process, 13, 16, 37; details of process, 37; hand combing, 37; guild of combers, 38, 43, 44; invention of machine combing, 54, 69, 118; strike (1825), 124

Condenser, machine in woollen-yarn production, 72, 94; description of, 149; in Pudsey, 187
Cookson, Ronald of Holbeck, 51
Coops, Joseph of Pudsey, 50
Cotton, price of, 73; use in worsted manufacture, 74; trade of Great Britain, numbers employed, 76; growing in United States, 79; proportion of men employed, 91; cotton warps, 109, 111, 149
Cotton spinning, development of, 42
Crabtree, John of Halifax, 23
Crompton, Samuel, 127
Crossband twist, 150
Crump, W. C., Leeds Woollen Industry, 50, 59, 60, 166
Curwen, E. Cecil, 55

Dalton, John, 7
Damask, description of, 150
Darney, W., The Progress of the Gospel in Yorkshire and other Parts (1751), 57
Defoe, Daniel, 28, 29, 30, 33, 44, 166; description of Yorkshire, 166 etc
Delaine, 150
Denisons, Messrs, 52
Design, development of in woollen cloth, 110; copying of in West Riding, 136; effect of blending different fibres, 132
Devil, machine for opening wool, 72
Dewing process, description of, 151
Dewsbury, 98; manufacture of shoddy at, 101, 104, 111, 115; average earnings at, 115
Dictionary of National Biography, on Baines, 8
Dimity, 151
Dobbies, 151
Dolphin Holme, first worsted spinning by machinery at, 123
Domestic system of clothmaking, 20; Yorkshire's position in 18th century, 33; responds to 18th century expansion, 35; effect of Parliamentary Reports (1806), 50, 71
Don Quixote, 17
Donnisthorpe, inventor of combing

INDEX

tion, 108; wool for worsteds, 124
Woollen trade, Great Britain, numbers employed in, 76; progress of, 81 et seq; number of manufacturers, 90; proportion of men employed, 91; number supported by, 92; estimated annual value of, 103 et seq; factories in 1870, 114; changes in Pudsey, 172 et seq
Woollen trade, Yorkshire, development of rural trade, 16 et seq; size of trade in 15th century, 19; clothmaking in 16th century, 19 et seq; in 18th century, 23 et seq; trading conditions in 17th century, 24; domestic system in, 33 et seq; industrial revolution in, 46 et seq; government's opinion of woollen workers, 49-50; Benjamin Gott and, 51 et seq; slow mechanisation of, 70; processes of manufacture in, 72 et seq; compared with other textile industries, 74 et seq; geographical distribution of, 83; number of factories, 91; supplementary account to 1870, 106 et seq
Woollen and worsted trade compared, 36, 69 et seq; number of factories in 19th century compared, 76; exports, 86; workers in woollen and worsted manufacture, 88 et seq
Wormald & Fountain, 52

Worsted Acts (1777), 122
Worsted trade, development of in Yorkshire, 30; in Yorkshire in 18th century, 35 et seq; effect of new spinning machinery, 39; development of roller spinning in, 40; pioneers of worsted trade, 45; increase of factories, 74; use of cotton warp, 74; number employed in manufacture, 76, 85; proportion of men employed, 91; number of people supported by, 92; account of, 118 et seq; improvements in manufacture, 125; excessive drinking in Yorkshire, 138; Forbes' estimate, 139; James' estimate, 140; Behrens' estimate, 141; wages in Halifax district, 142; in Bradford district, 143
Worsted trade of Great Britain, numbers employed, 85
Wyatt, James, 126

Yarmouth, 119
Yarn, export statistics, 81
York, medieval clothmaking, 12; weavers' guild, 12; decline in cloth trade, 18
Yorkshire wool trial (1613), 25; second trial (1637), 27; third trial (1676), 28

199